Bully-Proofing Your Child:
A Family Guide

Carla Garrity, Ph.D. • William Porter, Ph.D.
Mitchell Baris, Ph.D.

D1468679

ISBN-13: 978-1503006348
ISBN-10: 1503006344

Acknowledgements

This book grew from over twenty years of listening to and engaging with children as they described bullying, taunting, ridicule and a fear of harm at school, in sports programs and, nowadays, over the internet as well. The authors began developing educational programs to bring safety and comfort to the students of this world. The result was *The Bully-Proofing Your School* series of books. Enormous appreciation for years of shared learning goes to our fellow authors and colleagues:

- Nancy Sager, Kayla McCarnes and Karin Nelson who authored *Bully-Proofing in Early Childhood*

- Kathryn Jens, Nancy Sager and Cam Short-Camilli who joined with us in writing *Bully-Proofing: The Elementary Years*

- Marla Bonds and Sally Stoker who wrote *Bully-Proofing: The Middle School Years*

- Sally Stoker and Jill McDonald who co-authored *Bully-Proofing: The High School Years*

The landscape of bullying has changed since we first began our work in this area. It is no longer about just the bully and the victim. We now know that this is a comprehensive and complicated dynamic where many factors interweave: the temperament of the children, the climate of the school, the interplay of technology and the attitude of the family and surrounding community. We thank our colleague Dorothy Espelage for her ongoing support and research in this area.

Our loudest thank you goes to the children who were brave enough to share their stories and to believe there were adults who would help them. We learned early on that the children knew the most.

Betsy Kummer, our outstanding editor, designer, creative thinker and colleague, brought all of our words together into this book. Thank you, Betsy.

About the Authors

Carla Garrity, Ph.D. and William Porter, Ph.D. authored, with three of their colleagues, *The Bully-Proofing Your School* curriculum guides for the elementary years. Mitchell Baris, Ph.D., a family psychologist, joined them for this companion book which grew out of the questions and concerns of families wanting greater understanding and strategies for bully-proofing their children.

All three authors have worked in schools, communities, sports programs and with families to assure that all children have the opportunity to learn and play in environments that promote healthy interactions.

Table of Contents

Families must advocate for their children as bullying is a complex dynamic that requires a multi-faceted intervention approach. There are no magical answers. The best remedy is to understand the dynamics and build, with your child, a personal strategy.

Bully-Proofing Your Child: A Family Guide will offer you the means for building a comprehensive strategy for your child. You will learn:

- How to assess the climate at your child's school or program

- How to evaluate your child's vulnerabilities

- Tools for determining your child's temperament and competencies

- How to approach the school and develop a plan to create a focus on a positive climate

- How to deal with cyberbullying

- Knowledge and tools for empowering your child

- How to reshape bullying behavior

Part I:
Bullying Fundamentals

- **Understanding Bullying**
- **Gender Differences: How Boys Bully & How Girls Bully**
- **Is It Bullying or Normal Conflict?**

Chapter 1

Understanding Bullying

Bullying is about the abuse of power. Many students enjoy commanding personal power. There is nothing wrong with this unless this student is using power to intimidate, harass, or gain an advantage over another. Bullying begins in the early childhood years, peaks in middle school, and ebbs during high school. Bullying behavior causes pain that can last for years. Often no one helps in bullying situations. When they do, research shows that other children are more likely to intervene than adults.

Bullying behavior is a type of aggression that:

- Can take **many different forms** (verbal, physical, or social)
- Can occur either in person or via electronic means
- Can be done by an individual or a group
- Is often, though not always, **repeated** over time
- Is done on purpose, with the **intent** to cause harm
- Occurs when there is an **imbalance of power** between the student who is targeted and the student who is the aggressor
- More frequently targets students who are **perceived as different**, based on their class, race, religion, gender, sexuality, appearance, behavior or ability, and are not in supportive environments

5

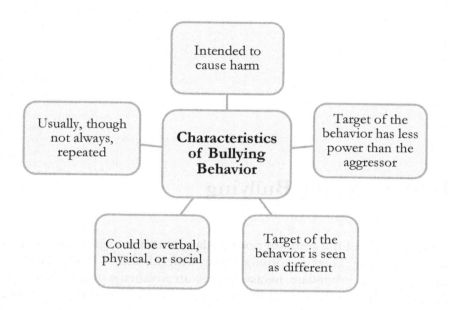

Let's look at how bullying occurs. Not all children get bullied. Most children report that they are teased, called names, or excluded from time to time, but they bounce back and tend not to become repeat targets of bullies.

Bullies find a certain type of child and focus their negative power wielding on them.

Who does the bully find for a target?

In essence, children are at risk to be bullied when they appear vulnerable. Many things can make a child seem this way. Physical characteristics, such as weight, size, disabilities, or coordination problems, can make an individual child stand out. This, however, is not the most important factor. The most important factor that makes a child a target is the way he or she responds to taunting. Appearing anxious, afraid, helpless, and unlikely to fight back can place a child at risk. This emotional vulnerability creates an easy target for the bully to abuse and mistreat. Vulnerable children include:

1. Shy and withdrawn children. These are children who are shy, insecure, cry easily and lack social skills. Often they have few friends and play alone at recess time, which makes them easy targets, as no one is nearby to hear or help. They are frequently too fragile to stick up for themselves. They, honestly, are afraid of the bully and the bully knows that. These children convey their fear through their bodies. Many of them have no idea how to enter a group. They walk with their heads down and their shoulders slumped and make no eye contact. They are easy for the bully to spot and they make prime targets. Bullies are stimulated by the emotional response of these children.

2. Special needs children. Special-needs children may have a learning style difference, a physical disability or be easy to arouse emotionally. Some studies have found that almost five times as many special-needs children are the targets of bullies than their classmates.

3. Children who do not fit the social norm in a specific setting. Some settings are diverse and inclusive while others are so homogeneous that a child not fitting the norm stands out and is easy to target. Inherent factors that make a child vulnerable include race, sexual orientation, religion, gender, size, weight and even food allergies.

4. Quick-to-react and highly emotional children. These children are almost the opposite of shy children. They are usually right in the middle of the action on the playground. Often restless and action oriented, they are likely to burst into the middle of games others are playing. They are rarely alone or quiet. They like interaction and seek it out. Sometimes they push, shove, or use other aggressive tactics to get attention. Nasty remarks burst out of their mouths without thinking. They rarely respect rules or boundaries, wanting to be noticed. Not surprisingly, these children irritate and annoy other children.

At first, you may think a quick-to-react child is a bully. If you don't look closely, they can appear the same. There are three characteristics, however, that are important in telling the difference between a bully and an over reactive child:

a) An over reactive child is not purposefully mean or malicious. This type of child is impulsive, but when he or she realizes that another child has been hurt, sympathy and/or empathy is felt and typically the over reactive child will apologize. The reactive child acts without thinking but does not intend to hurt another.

b) This type of child is not as quick witted, mean spirited, or as cunning as the bully. The bully will overpower this child and win.

c) A bully has friends; a quick to react child tends to have few or no friends.

d) They are fair game for bullies because of their impulsive behavior and bullies use this to justify their behavior.

Why would a bully pick on an easy-to-arouse child? There are many answers. One is that these children often irritate others and the bully wants to show who is boss. A bully can justify picking on a child who is irritating. Targeting an over reactive child creates a lot of attention on the playground or in group settings. Unlike the shy child, who cries and trembles, these children fight back with a great deal of gusto and noise. This attracts attention. Other children come running over to see what the commotion is all about. Soon a crowd has gathered to watch. This

 both stimulates and satisfies the bully's need for power and domination.

Bullies like having power and will frequently prey on the same children, time and time again. An unfortunate situation often develops on the playground when this happens as other children begin to gather and watch; some actually experience excitement from the drama and action. Others join in to gain approval. Bullying is exciting news on the childhood playground scene. Being part of the action may even be appealing, and other children may decide to join in. A contagion effect begins to happen. Soon the bully has far more children on his or her side and the target feels even more helpless. When a scene such as this plays itself out day after day, the victimized child grows more miserable, desperate, and incapable of handling the situation. If the cycle has grown this serious, it will not turn itself around without adult help.

Who Are the Bullies?

Many people have this image of a bully: a bully is usually a boy, physically large, a poor student, and basically insecure. All of these are completely false. Bullies are not all boys; girls are bullies as well. Bullies are typically average students and are not failing school. Low self-esteem is not a problem for a bully. In fact, most bullies have an inflated image of themselves. They enjoy the power that aggression brings and they feel entitled to recognition, privilege, and special treatment. Bullies thrive on targeting easy-to-arouse children. It is personality style, not size or gender that defines a bully. Many are verbally competent and liked by teachers and others.

A typical bully is a child who:

1. Values power and the rewards that aggression can bring.
2. Lacks compassion and empathy for others.
3. Lacks guilt for his or her actions.
4. Sincerely believes that it is okay to treat others in a cruel fashion.
5. Likes to dominate and be in charge.
6. Thinks it is okay to be abusive in order to get whatever he or she wants.
7. Avoids adults and plays out of the sight of adult eyes.
8. Has strong verbal skills and is verbally convincing.
9. Projects problems onto others, blames others and does not take ownership.

As a parent, you must appraise your child honestly. As difficult as it may be to admit, your child may be the bully claiming to be a victim in order to avoid responsibility for his or her behavior. Bullies are capable of manipulating their parents into believing that the problem is the other person's fault.

The outcome in life is very poor for children who are bullies. These children are three times more likely to have committed a crime by early adulthood. They are less likely to finish college, maintain a job, or establish a good marriage. Girls who bully are more likely to raise children who will bully. None of this needs to happen. Bullies as well as victims can have the opportunity to be productive and happy adults if their personalities are recognized early in childhood and redirected. The rest of the book will help you in rating your own child and redirecting him or her to a healthy pathway.

ACTIVITY

Ask your child, "Do others sometimes pick on you?"

If the answer is "Nobody picks on me," you may have a child who is a bully. Bullies will not admit to even occasional run-ins with other kids.

Now try a second question: "How do you feel when you see someone else getting picked on?"

If the answer is "He probably got what he deserved," then you must look further into your child's behavior. Most children feel badly when they see another child being picked on, even though they may not be brave enough to do anything or to confront the bully. Children who lack this feeling for others are at risk for doing emotional or physical harm because they cannot relate to the feelings another child experiences. A bully's desire for power outweighs the reward for compassion.

Chapter 2

Gender Differences: How Boys Bully and How Girls Bully

Both boys and girls bully. While boys are more likely to use or threaten physical aggression, girls may use gossiping, whispering, threats, and spreading rumors to hurt others. The abuse is more emotional than physical but girls report that it hurts just as much, if not more, than being hit.

Bullying Behavior

The Bullying Behaviors Chart on page 12 shows four different styles of bullying. Girls tend to use social alienation and intimidation. Boys are more likely to use physical or verbal aggression. Notice that there is a scale across the top ranging from mild to severe. Targeted children are different in how much of this aggression they can tolerate. Some children get very upset with mild bullying. These children:

- Are often alone, shy, or have few friends.
- May have a learning disability and do not easily or quickly process social cues.
- Have been bullied in the past.
- Have suffered a trauma such as a death, divorce, or other significant loss.
- Are physically weak and cannot defend themselves.

Bullying Baheviors Chart

Mild		Moderate			Severe
←					→

Physical Aggression

•Pushing •Shoving •Spitting	•Kicking •Hitting	•Defacing property •Stealing	•Physical acts that are demeaning and humiliating but not bodily harmful (e.g., de-panting) •Locking in a closed or confined space	•Physical violence against family or friends	•Threatening with a weapon •Inflicting bodily harm

Social Alienation (in person or through social media)

•Gossiping •Causing embarrass-ment	•Setting up to look foolish •Spreading rumors about	•Ethnic slurs •Setting up to take the blame	•Publicly humiliating (e.g., revealing personal information via social media) •Excluding from group •Social rejection	•Maliciously excluding •Manipulating social order to achieve rejection •Malicious rumor-mongering	•Threatening with total isolation from peer group

Verbal Aggression

•Mocking •Name calling •Dirty looks •Taunting	•Teasing about clothing or possessions	•Teasing about appearance	•Intimidating text messages, emails, or phone calls	•Verbal threats to steal or damage property or possessions	•Verbal threats of violence or of inflicting bodily harm

Intimidation

•Threatening to reveal personal information •Graffiti •Publicly challenging to do something	•Defacing property or clothing •Playing a dirty trick	•Taking possessions (e.g., lunch, clothing, toys)	•Extortion •Sexual/racial taunting	•Threats of using coercion against family or friends	•Coercion •Threatening with a weapon

Girl Bullying

Girls tend to bully in a subtle and indirect manner using "relational aggression" tactics – including name calling, exclusion, gossip, manipulation, and threats to social status – to cause harm (Crick & Grotpeter, 1995). One girl, or a group of girls, might walk up to a target and tell her that her hair is an ugly color or that her clothes are not in fashion. The put-downs are usually about clothing, hair, or overall appearance. By third to fourth grade, the tactics change. Girls often form cliques or groups and stand together, taunting or harassing the victim. This is often done at recess or lunchtime and in a discreet manner so adults do not notice. Some girls take it a step further and promise that the excluded girl can be part of their group if she does something for them. This may be bringing them money or food. It could also include something humiliating or embarrassing they ask her to do. Too often, targets believe this will truly buy them a chance to be "in," and they do what is asked only to find the bullying does not stop.

Put-Downs

**Network
or Group
Bullying**

Gossiping

Social Alienation

By fifth to sixth grade, the situation grows more serious. A victimized girl may find she is receiving intimidating or threatening notes that warn her that something bad will happen. Gossiping and spreading very damaging and embarrassing stories are commonplace. With the internet, these tactics are even easier to use, require no face-to-face contact, and spread quickly. Overall, girls use networking, put-downs, humiliation and exclusion. In recent years, however, the use of physical aggression by girls has been increasing.

Boy Bullying

Boys are less likely to change their tactics as they grow older. Throughout childhood, boys typically bully with physical aggression or by threatening to use physical aggression. Exclusion may also be used as in athletics when someone says, "Does he have to play?" Most of the time, however, boy bullying is a quick jab, push or shove, elbow or knee,

15

or head thrust into a wall or locker. Whatever it is, it hurts. It is also quick and over before anyone sees what is happening. The bully's size or strength is intimidating. Boys bully by creating fear and an always present threat of physical harm. Boys see bullies as large, strong, and powerful. The drawing of a bully by a boy shows a bully who is intimidating physically because of his size or strength.

Threats of Aggression

How Bullies Find a Target

It is fairly easy for a bully to find a victim. Recall that bullies are impulsive, lack empathy, and have a strong need to dominate others. They like having power. Finding someone who will not fight back, is alone, or lacks social skills, is an easy way for the bully to feel very powerful. Picking on a competent child with a circle of friends is far harder. The bully might not come away the winner. Looking foolish is not something the bully will risk. Finding a sure and easy target is the best way for a bully to let others know that he or she is in charge.

Chapter 3

Is It Bullying or Normal Conflict?

Far more families worry that their children are targeted than that their children will bully. Most children complain from time to time about harassment and teasing from others. Anger and hurtful remarks are part of conflict at all ages. It is important to know how children of different ages play together. Bully/victim problems become more serious and change as children grow older. Bullying requires adult intervention so recognizing the difference is critical.

In this chapter you will learn how to tell the difference between bullying and normal conflict between children. Sometimes what sounds worrisome to a family is just normal peer conflict and sometimes it is the beginning of a true bully problem. There are three basic ways to know if your child is truly being bullied:

1. The bully picks on your child with intent to cause harm or gain power. Typically the negative action is repeated over and over again.

2. The bully wins because your child is smaller, younger, or less socially able to cope.

3. Your child is afraid and very upset. The bully sees it all as "no big deal" or as "deserved." The bully actually enjoys upsetting your child.

Why such meanness? How can we fortify our children against this? There are no simple answers. Conflict between children who interact together is inevitable. It is part of learning how to have relationships, how to share, compromise, and work together cooperatively. This does not just come naturally. Children go through stages of social development.

How children handle their differences shifts as they grow older. Parents who understand this sequence can help teach at these moments of conflict during normal play be it with a friend or with a sibling. Recent studies have revealed that bully/target dynamics exist between siblings where one child in a family may be repeatedly and unmercifully put down, teased or abused physically. Children who have good role models for problem-solving are far less likely to be either a target or a bully.

Ages 3 to 5

Preschoolers play beside each other but not in a give-and-take fashion. Watch two three-year olds with a box of building blocks. They will most likely each be building their own structure but with one pile of shared blocks. Play will go happily until one of them takes the last block or takes the block the other one needs or wants. The child who lost out will most likely grab the block or begin yelling loudly. Asking, sharing, and self-regulation are skills that three-year olds can master if modeled and taught.

What can the family do?

1. Give a clear message that hurting others is not okay. Teach compassion.
2. State that there are consequences for biting, hitting, throwing, or hurting a friend.
3. Offer a fair solution. For example, say "Hitting will not get you a turn on the tricycle. After (name) rides around the playground one time, then it will be your turn."
4. Help put the solution into action.

Ages 5 and 6

At this age, kids still fight over toys and possessions, but now they add verbal insults and put-downs. They want their own way, to have the first turn, or to play with a toy as long as they want. If they don't win, they threaten, they tattle, and then they act mean. By this age, children have figured out that they are more likely to win if an adult does not see what they are doing. Few feel guilty for long, but both guilt and empathy are emerging at this age, as is some sense of turn taking. Seeing another child's pain and responding to it is a positive sign. A child who shows no awareness of another's feelings may be on the road to becoming a bully. A child who gives up, gives in, and tattles but never sticks up for his or her rights may end up being a bully's target.

What can the family do?

1. Teach social skills—how to join in, stand up for others, and demonstrate kindness.

2. Role play ways to help other kids and have actual face-to-face conversations.

3. Teach how to approach others. Develop a plan. Look for someone alone or a group of three or more children to join. A group of two children playing together is the hardest group to join. Do not ask, "Can I play?" as typically this question will result in exclusion. Just join in without disrupting the flow of the play.

4. Build ideas for how to ask for needs to be met. Point out the pain caused to the other child. For example, say "You go first this time but I get to go first next time." or "Please, may I have the swing when you're done." Connect the actions and consequences—"He is crying because you pushed him off the swing and took it."

Ages 6 to 8

This is the age of games and sports with rules. Self-control is being learned and rules help to enforce the concepts of fairness, taking turns, and sharing. The world, however, is still black and white to a six-year old. Either you broke the rule or you didn't; there is little gray. Children take one side or the other; it is either right or it is wrong.

Being good at something is terribly important at this age. Sports and athletics are where many children spend their free time. Parents who have unathletic children need to work to find other outlets for their children. Teasing over being inferior is so commonplace that it is almost an invitation to ridicule to place a child in an activity he or she cannot master. For unathletic children, find activities that reward participation not excellence. Power is important in the six-to eight-year-old peer group, and kids vie for it. Size, strength, and agility will typically assure a boy of a power position in his peer culture.

Girls win power through social connections. Putting down a girl and excluding her for her clothing or looks is quite common. The girl delivering the put-down often gains prestige and position in the peer group and takes one more rival out of the loop. Tattling, distorting the truth, and gossiping are all part of the playground culture of six-to eight-year-old girls. Sadly, assuring this status in the peer group takes precedence for some children over and above protecting another from rejection. Group affiliation is the hallmark of middle childhood. Differences are a disadvantage and similarities are emphasized.

What can the family do?

1. Have conversations about how your child can support others.

2. Families need to listen during the drive to and from school, at sporting events, and at parties.

3. Establish guidelines and boundaries around internet, cell phone and media use. Being aware of your child's online activities is essential. Families differ in how sophisticated they are with technology and how invasive or restrictive they are comfortable being but opting out and completely ignoring this important aspect of your child's social life is not a wise choice.

4. Opportunities to teach problem solving are plentiful at this age and will set a foundation for life. Take time to talk to and teach your child about:

   - Acceptance of diversity.
   - How to say "no" in a kind way.
   - Making an effort to include other children.
   - Developing compassion and empathy.
   - Awareness of others' feelings.
   - Finding outcomes that benefit everyone.
   - Not bullying back, but sticking up for himself or herself.

Ages 9 to 11

The world rapidly shifts to gray for children at about age nine. Problems no longer have simple black and white solutions. Complexities creep in, value judgments are made, and issues of morals and justice matter. Children worry about "what is fair." This is when compromise begins, which is sacrificing something for the good of the team or the relationship. This is not turn-taking—"You first today and me tomorrow and everything will be even." Compromise is: "I give up some of what I want and you give up some of what you want so we can reach a goal and preserve our relationship." The message is that the relationship matters as much or more than individual needs and wants.

This takes maturity. A child must know and recognize his or her own feelings, have empathy for the feelings of others, and be able to regulate strong emotions. These are the building blocks for relationships in jobs and families later in life. Bullies usually do not master these steps. Targeted children, on the other hand, are so eager for a relationship that they may sacrifice themselves in the process. Neither is healthy. Teach your child a balance between looking out for his or her needs yet respecting those of others.

What can the family do?

1. Talk about the importance of compromise.

2. Take real-life examples (such as a call a referee made that was controversial, information out of the daily news, or court cases) and discuss the viewpoint of both sides.

3. Model good problem-solving in your own life and family.

4. Establish family rituals that promote fun, bonding, and service to others. (For example, shovel the snow of an elderly neighbor's sidewalk, regularly make a family meal, or volunteer as a family.)

Ages 11 to 13

This stage of a young person's life is characterized by a search for identity. This can be one of the most challenging stages of development. Finding a group that fits is crucial. Boys are seeking groups that reflect their interests, activities and behavior. Girls are typically focused on social relationships. They are acutely aware of who is "in", who is "out", and there is often much drama.

What can the family do?

1. Increasingly schools offer a wide array of extra-curricular groups; however, for some adolescents finding a group within the school setting may be a struggle. You may need to look outside of school as well.

2. Some adolescents are not developing in-person social communication skills because they spend far too much of their time playing video games. Encourage some involvement in groups that require verbal communication.

3. Have a conversation with your child about the different groups or "cliques" that are in the school or program. Who are the members of these groups? How are these groups perceived by students? How are these groups perceived by your child?

4. Codes to communicate are commonplace in text messaging and on the internet. Learn all about these codes as some of them focus on violence, sex and drugs. This special lingo of the adolescent can be found by searching the internet.

5. Peer pressure is intense in these years. Adolescents may reject the values of their family and instead align with the values of a peer group. Stay attuned to your child's choice of peer groups.

6. Practice how to join in while keeping emotions in check.

Ages 14 to 18

By the high school years, adolescents are succumbing far less to peer pressure. They are typically developing a sense of self that is defined by their own values, ethics and interests. Issues are thought through and respect for diversity, rather than conformity, increases. Adolescents recognize the vulnerabilities of others and can reflect on social justice issues. Talking with family members about issues in the news, in school, and with friends helps in learning the complexities of compromise and the viewpoints of both sides of a dilemma. During this stage of your child's development, discuss diversity – along racial, ethnic, economic, sexual, and gender lines.

By high school, adolescents have typically found one or more groups, clubs or outside interests. If your child has not, this is reason for concern. Discuss ways to connect with others who enjoy similar activities.

What can the family do?

1. Listen, be supportive and express concern if you become aware of unwise choices.
2. Sexual and romantic relationships are developing. Be alert to any signs of sexual harassment and/or dating violence.
3. Support your child's interests by showing up at events even if the event is not something you enjoy.
4. Teach your adolescent assertive solutions if aggression or emotional intimidation is occurring.
5. Talk about stereotypes and encourage respect for differences and diversity.
6. Remember that relationships are intense and break-ups are tough.

Table 2 summarizes the typical conflicts at each age and possible resolutions.

Table 2: Conflict and Resolution

Age	Typical Conflict	Preferred Style of Resolution
3-5 years	• Conflict likely over toys, possessions ("It's mine") or going first	• Action oriented • Separate the children • Change the topic • No-nonsense, direct and concise
5-6 years	• Selfishness, wanting own way • Threatening with tattling or not playing again ("I'm not inviting you to my birthday.")	• Connect actions and consequences • Undo what the offender did • No-nonsense or problem solving
6-8 years	• What is fair and what isn't • Teasing, gossiping, feeling superior • Putting down, accusing of something not true or distorted	• Mutual negotiation with help • Understanding of others' intentions • Problem-solving
9-11 years	• Bossiness, tattling, put-downs, showing off, betrayal	• Building empathy • Talking things out • Negotiating • Compromising
11 to 13 years	• Inclusion/exclusion in groups • Shifting group allegiance • Peer pressure	• Verbal negotiation • Compromise • Finding confirming group
14 to 18 years	• Stereotypes, prejudices, judgments • Sexuality and relationships	• Affirming sense of self without hurting another • Increasing development of compassion and empathy • Awareness of unfairness and capacity to assert self

Remember that normal peer conflict is *not* bullying. Table 3 provides some guidance on understanding the important differences between the two.

Table 3: Recognizing the Difference

Normal Peer Conflict	Bullying
Equal power between friends	Imbalance of power
Individuals often play together	Individuals rarely play together
Happens occasionally	Repeated negative actions
Accidental	Purposeful
Not serious	Serious with threat of physical, emotional or social harm
Equal emotional reactions	Strong emotional reaction from victim and little or no emotional reaction from bully
Not seeking power or attention	Seeking power, control, or material things
Not trying to get something	Attempt to gain material things or power
Remorse – will take responsibility	No remorse. Blames the targeted child
Effort to solve the problem	No effort or interest in solving the problem

Part I of this book has introduced basic bullying concepts and provided general suggestions for responding to bullying when it occurs at various ages. But how else can you determine what your child needs? Part II delves more deeply into assessing your child's temperament and vulnerabilities.

Part II:
Assessing Your Child's Risk

- Assessing Your Child
- Assessing Climate
- Putting the Pieces Together

Bullying problems can be solved, but may require effort on several fronts. Bullying is a unique dynamic that starts with the bully, but also involves the targeted child's vulnerabilities, temperament, and climate (environment). This section will give you tools for understanding and rating all these factors. Then, you will use your assessment of these factors to determine your child's level of risk. It is important not to overreact to any one factor. Rather, consider how all three interact. Your assessment in this section will inform your action plan for your child, which you will develop in Part III.

Collect data and assess
VULNERABILITIES

Collect data and assess
TEMPERAMENT

Collect data and
assess **CLIMATE**

Develop **PLAN**

Some children will require more help than others. Some may be easily taught skills that offset risk factors, or skills to become upstanders. Some will benefit from collaboration between their families and school or program leaders. Some may need to change schools or settings. Again, all three areas, vulnerabilities, temperament, and climate, must be considered together because each is affected by the other two. For instance, temperament challenges or vulnerabilities pose a higher risk in an unsafe climate, but may not be a risk in a very caring and safe climate.

In the table below, the vulnerabilities are the same, but climate and skills lower the child's risk substantially. Be certain to consider developmental milestones discussed earlier in this book as you evaluate the three factors below.

Table 4: How Factors Interact

	Higher Risk	Lower Risk
Temperament *(Temperament can be offset by skills)*	• Shy child or often alone • Emotionally sensitive child	• Easy-going child • Socially-skilled child
Vulnerabilities *(Vulnerabilites are often unchangeable)*	• Child is different from the norm of the school or program	• Child "fits in" with the dominant norm of the school or program
Climate *(Climate can change)*	• Athletics highly valued • School is exclusive	• Many clubs and activities • School is inclusive

In Part III you will find skills and strategies to select from to best meet your child's needs based on your risk assessment. Families must reflect on where to draw the fine line between protecting a child and supporting growth through creative problem solving, which may include some discomfort.

Remember from Part I that bullying is about power, and power imbalance. Wanting power is often thought of as harmful to others as well as selfish — as negative only. This is not true. Most individuals wish to feel powerful. It is the manner in which someone seeks power that needs a closer look. Bullies seize power for themselves and enjoy the response they get from the children they target. Typically this is unearned power that harms and uses another. By contrast, there are healthy ways to feel powerful. For example, sharing a kindness or talent, learning a new skill, or giving a compliment can create feelings of power. Children who use power in healthy ways when exposed to bullying are often referred to as "upstanders." Essentially, an upstander is a child who recognizes a bullying situation and has the courage to "stand up" for the child who was targeted. Upstanders have power, but they use it in positive ways. After your risk assessment, if your child is not at high risk, or as part of your child's action plan, you can help your child develop upstander skills. In Part III you will find skills and strategies that can empower your child.

All the assessments in Part II are organized such that answers falling to the left are more negative indicators, and falling to the right are more positive indicators. (To the far right may be "not applicable" or "not available".) Some of the assessments also have open-ended questions.

As you complete the assessments in the following sections, keep in mind these important points:

- Conflict is not the same as bullying

- Having a bullying-prevention program in a school or community-based program is not a guarantee of a safe climate. Is the school or program taking deliberate steps to create a positive climate?

- The presence of friends and upstander children is a critical protective factor

- Stories portrayed in the media are unique to one situation and may not represent a comprehensive picture of your child's situation or needs

- Kids need to be able to list three to four adults who are available when and where needed, that they would talk to about problems.

Chapter 4

Assessing Your Child

Each child is unique, with his or her own vulnerabilities, temperament, and skills or strengths. This chapter will introduce you to some tools to help you better understand your child's vulnerabilities, which are frequently not in a child's control, and temperament and skills, which can often be shaped or developed.

Determining Your Child's Vulnerabilities

Vulnerabilities are characteristics that separate a child from her community of peers and from the norm of the group. These differences can be worth celebrating, may be part of a family's core values, and are largely things that cannot or should not be changed. However, these vulnerabilities may place a child at risk of being bullied. Some environments are more tolerant of differences than others. Each school and program has unique norms. Prejudices rarely change quickly or easily. Consequently, you will need to determine how far your child is removed from the average or norm for a particular environment. Use the Vulnerability Assessment on the next page to assess your child in the context of each program in which your child is involved. Make a copy for each program or school in which your child is involved.

> **Vulnerabilities:**
> *Characteristics that are known to be associated with being targeted for bullying — often these are ways in which the child differs from peers in a particular context.*

35

What you learn here about your child may also help determine what you ask and observe during your climate assessment, where you can focus your attention on how that environment responds to your child's particular vulnerabilities.

Vulnerability Assessment

Instructions: Consider the characteristics listed below and assess whether your child seems different from the majority of other children in a particular setting. Mark where your child fits on the continuum for each characteristic. Not all characteristics may be relevant to your child. Checks falling to the left of center indicate a higher risk than checks falling to the right.

Compared to the majority of children in this environment, my child is...

	Very Different ←————————————————————→ **Very Similar**
Religion	←————————————————————————→
Race/Ethnicity	←————————————————————————→
Socio economic	←————————————————————————→
Athletic interest/ability	←————————————————————————→
Art/cultural interest/ability	←————————————————————————→
Style of appearance (hygiene, clothing, tattoos, piercings)	←————————————————————————→
Visible disability	←————————————————————————→
Invisible disability (autism spectrum, ADD/ADHD, behavioral challenges, twice exceptional, past trauma)	←————————————————————————→
Physical appearance	←————————————————————————→
Academic emphasis/ability (giftedness, high performer; learning disability)	←————————————————————————→
Gender presentation	←————————————————————————→
Sexual orientation	←————————————————————————→
Size (height, weight)	←————————————————————————→

Rating Your Child's Temperament

Certain character traits or temperament challenges may make a child an easy target. By contrast, certain skills or strengths provide protection. Some children seem to have a natural tendency to stay calm, assured and unyielding. They are frequently described by their families as having these traits from early childhood. Other children, from early in life or as the result of a trauma, are easily stimulated, aroused, and reactive. Think of the traits on the right side of the midpoint as a shield that protects a child from being targeted. They are especially important for a child who has multiple vulnerabilities.

> ### *Temperament:*
> *Ways in which a child typically interacts with others and the world. Temperament may be fairly stable, but is also moldable through maturity and skill development.*

Temperament and Skills Assessment

Instructions: Assess your child by placing a checkmark along each of the arrows. The more marks that fall to the left of the midpoint, the greater the risk for the child. However, note that these are character traits which can be reshaped and taught as acquired skills, which will be the focus of Part III.

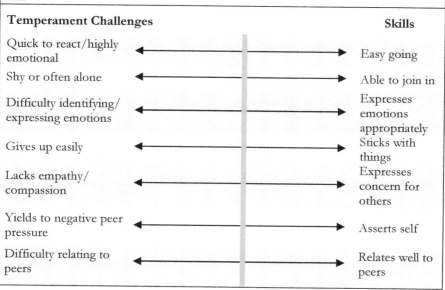

Temperament Challenges	Skills
Quick to react/highly emotional	Easy going
Shy or often alone	Able to join in
Difficulty identifying/expressing emotions	Expresses emotions appropriately
Gives up easily	Sticks with things
Lacks empathy/compassion	Expresses concern for others
Yields to negative peer pressure	Asserts self
Difficulty relating to peers	Relates well to peers

Chapter 5

Assessing Climate

It is important to evaluate the overall environment or "climate" of each particular program or school in which your child is involved; this may include any that you are considering for your child in the future. Consider athletic teams, summer camps, after school programs, and other similar types of activities. Copy the assessment on page 41 before completing it if you want to reuse it for assessing multiple programs.

Tolerant: *accepting of diversity, such as differences that are physical, behavioral, or in beliefs (opposite: Intolerant)*

Inclusive: *welcoming and including diverse individuals and groups equally in activities, not leaving any out (opposite: Exclusive)*

This assessment on page 41 is meant as a guide, not a prescription. There is no exact cut off for a good or bad school or program. Find more people to talk to, or observe some more, until you are satisfied that you have enough information to evaluate the program or school's climate. Keep in mind that the climate is only one part of the picture, as it interacts with your child's vulnerabilities and temperament.

Answers falling to the left are more negative indicators, and falling to the right are more positive indicators. (To the far right is 'not applicable' or 'not available'.) In general, a positive and safe climate is tolerant and inclusive. In addition, a positive climate includes activities and efforts that recognize all students.

Questions to Ask About the Program or School

While there may be a difference between policy and practice, the following questions may help you assess whether bullying prevention is a priority in the program or school, as one indicator of climate. Keep in mind who your source is, and what that person's perspective or role may be. Actual observation will be even more valuable, when possible. Also, consider having multiple sources. For example, after asking an administrator these questions, see if you can ask another parent the same questions. Use the assessment tool as a catalyst for constructive conversation with the school or program.

Climate Assessment 1: Interview

	N=No, Y=Yes, N/A= not applicable or no data			
1.	Are there one or two adults my child can identify as someone he/she can talk to about problems?	N	Y	N/A
2.	Are there one or two staff members that you trust and feel you can work with to address bullying issues?	N	Y	N/A
3.	Is bullying considered distinct from normal conflict?	N	Y	N/A
4.	Is there a bullying and harassment policy?	N	Y	N/A
5.	Is transportation covered in the policy?	N	Y	N/A
6.	Are cyberbullying and safe online practices covered in the policy?	N	Y	N/A
7.	Is there a procedure for me or my child to report an incident?	N	Y	N/A
8.	Are records kept of bullying and harassment incidents?	N	Y	N/A
9.	Is there a dedicated committee to promote a positive climate?	N	Y	N/A
10.	Is there a specific schedule for meetings regarding bullying prevention, and review of bully-prevention data and results?	N	Y	N/A
11.	Is there a character development or social skills curriculum?	N	Y	N/A
12.	Is there planned time for professional development for adults to learn about positive school climate and curriculum delivery?	N	Y	N/A
13.	Are there plans to maintain the focus on positive climate? (i.e. lessons, meetings, assemblies, events, or service projects)	N	Y	N/A
14.	Are there a variety of ways for students to engage positively? (i.e. academics, art, music, athletics, clubs, groups, events)	N	Y	N/A
15.	Is there a PTA, or other ways that families are included and involved?	N	Y	N/A
16.	Is there planned time for educating families about bullying prevention and how to support their students?	N	Y	N/A
17.	If this is a middle or high school, is there a GSA (Gay-Straight Alliance) or GLBTQ support group?	N	Y	N/A

Open-ended:

- How do you put your bully-prevention policies into practice?

- How does this program include minorities such as
_____?
(You may want to focus on your own child's vulnerabilities identified in the Assessing Your Child section).

- How do leaders or teachers deal with bullying or harassment?

- If my family reported an incident, what kind of follow-up should we expect?

- What specific bully-prevention goals does this program have, and how does the leadership plan to achieve them?

- Ask a program/school leader to define the difference between bullying and harassment.

- How are all students/groups included in the fabric of the school community?

Questions to Ask Your Child and Family

If your child is already involved in this program or school, ask yourself or your child these questions. If you are deciding if this program is right for your child, it is helpful to ask other families whose children already attend this school or program, when possible. If you have access to another family, remember to also ask the questions about the program, above. Again, keep in mind the source of the information, and, when possible, ask multiple sources.

Climate Assessment 2: Family Experience in this Program

	N=No, Y=Yes, N/A= not applicable or no data			
1.	Is your child excited or happy to go to this school or program?	N	Y	N/A
2.	Does your child feel that other children at the school or program are accepting (or inclusive), or does your child have friends there?	N	Y	N/A
3.	Does your child feel that adults at the program care about him or her?	N	Y	N/A
4.	Does your child have at least two adults he/she could turn to if there were a problem?	N	Y	N/A
5.	Do the adults in the program treat all children fairly?	N	Y	N/A
6.	Does your child feel safe in this program or school?	N	Y	N/A
7.	Does this program help your child feel included in the school community?	N	Y	N/A
8.	Does the child and/or family feel welcome at this program?	N	Y	N/A
9.	Do the staff and families work together respectfully?	N	Y	N/A
10.	Are there adults in this school or program that the family feels they can approach about problems?	N	Y	N/A
11.	Are there adults in this school or program that the family trusts?	N	Y	N/A
12.	Are there adults in this school or program that the family feels are helpful in resolving problems?	N	Y	N/A
13.	If bullying or harassment occurred – were you satisfied with how the program addressed it?	N	Y	N/A

Open-ended:

- What types of positive interactions have you seen in this program?

- How does the school or program go about developing a positive climate?

- What types of negative interactions, such as bullying, have you seen in this program?

Observation

Your own direct observation of the program or school can be invaluable. Sometimes this can be accomplished largely while waiting to visit a program leader, or when picking up or dropping off your child. Or, you may be allowed to take a tour, attended or unattended. For the safety of children, make sure to follow the program or school policy regarding visitors.

Climate Assessment 3: Direct Observation

1=mostly not true, 2= sometimes true, 3=frequently true, 4=almost always true *N/A= not applicable or no data*						

In common areas (school grounds, halls, cafeterias):

1.	Students' language is respectful and friendly to each other (no name-calling, swearing, put downs)	1	2	3	4	N/A
2.	Student movement is safe, without physical encounters with others	1	2	3	4	N/A
3.	Students are in mixed groups, and include students who come up to join in. *(Note: Pay special attention to the cafeteria and playground when observing this.)*	1	2	3	4	N/A
4.	Students with visible differences (disabilities, heavier, taller, or dressed differently) are included in groupings rather than alone	1	2	3	4	N/A
5.	Students engage in helping behaviors	1	2	3	4	N/A
6.	Adults are available and supervising	1	2	3	4	N/A
7.	Adults are respectful and positive with students	1	2	3	4	N/A
8.	Adults intervene when inappropriate behavior is seen	1	2	3	4	N/A
9.	Adults are respectful and positive with other adults	1	2	3	4	N/A
10.	The environment appears clean and respected (no graffiti, vandalism, trash)	1	2	3	4	N/A
11.	Expectations for behavior are posted on the wall and regularly reinforced in a positive manner by staff	1	2	3	4	N/A
12.	Displays value a variety of student groups and efforts (academics, art, music, athletics, classes, clubs)	1	2	3	4	N/A
13.	Displays, posters, and images include diversity (people of various ethnicities, appearances, disabilities, or genders)	1	2	3	4	N/A

In classrooms or groups:

14.	Students speak and listen respectfully	1	2	3	4	N/A
15.	Students engage in tasks presented by adults	1	2	3	4	N/A
16.	Students work in collaborative groups	1	2	3	4	N/A
17.	Students engage in helping behaviors	1	2	3	4	N/A
18.	Students and adults engage in problem-solving when conflict arises	1	2	3	4	N/A
19.	Adults speak respectfully and positively with students	1	2	3	4	N/A
20.	Adults address students by name (know names)	1	2	3	4	N/A
21.	The classroom has a uniform and articulated classroom management strategy	1	2	3	4	N/A

Chapter 6

Putting the Pieces Together

Once you have completed all three assessments – related to climate, vulnerabilities, and temperament – you are ready to pull them together for the complete risk assessment. All three of these factors shape a child's level of risk. Place a check mark in the following boxes to determine your child's level of risk. Again, remember that this is meant as a guide, not an absolute – you know your child best!

Risk Assessment

	Level of Risk	
	High Risk	**Low Risk**
Vulnerabilities: From the Vulnerability Assessment *(How many marks are to the left?)*	☐ Many	☐ Few
Temperament Challenges: From the Temperament and Skills Assessment *(Where do the marks fall?)*	☐ More on Left	☐ More on Right
Climate: From the Climate Assessment *(Overall impression.)*	☐ Intolerant/ Exclusive	☐ Tolerant/ Inclusive

---

Red Flags

1. If you checked all the boxes under the high risk column, your child is critically vulnerable.

2. If both climate and vulnerabilities are high risk, it is unlikely that you, as a family, can effectively provide safety in your child's social environment. You need to seriously consider whether an alternative school/program would be preferable for your child. On the other hand, the risk will be lessened if your child has friends and if the school or program has protective adults and upstander children.

In Part III you will develop a plan for your child, selecting from a variety of possible solutions based on your overall risk assessment, as well as the specific assessments of climate, vulnerabilities, and temperament that you conducted.

Part III:

Finding Solutions and Developing a Plan

- Changing Your Child's Environment
- When to Change Schools or Programs
- Empowering Your Child
- Learning Protective Strategies

Introduction

Armed with greater awareness of the situation and your child, you can now develop a plan. In doing so, you will consider two types of actions: changing the situation and empowering your child. Based on your assessment in Part II, you will identify and choose from a range of options in this two-pronged approach. You will seek balance between protecting your child and providing opportunities for growth.

Part III guides you in making decisions about what approaches do *not* work, which approaches *may* work, and what you can do to empower your child to better handle bullying situations. It will also cover how to build on your child's strengths, and when a change of school or program is an unfortunate necessity for the good of the child. We will conclude with how to turn a bystander into an upstander.

Chapter 7

Changing Your Child's Environment

Once you have evaluated your child and the situation, the most productive next step is to use the knowledge you now have as an empowered parent in approaching the school or program. This is especially important for the future well-being of your child if you determined that your child was high risk in terms of vulnerabilities and temperament. Regardless of whether the school or program has a bullying prevention program, the real key is creating an inclusive climate by shifting the silent majority into a caring majority, or "bystanders" into "upstanders". This requires adult leadership. Adults working together benefit students the most both academically and socially/emotionally. How you approach the school or program is critical.

For some parents, working with the school or program is not a comfortable option. You may have experienced dismissive, racist, opinionated, or other unfair treatment at school when you were a student. Or you may have already tried to approach the school on behalf of your child only to feel blamed or unheard or received a dismissive assurance that they are on top of the problem and have a bully program in place. Approaching the school or program is not your only choice, but is a way to influence and change the environment rather than try to effect change solely through the child. It is also a way for parents to make a positive contribution, not only to their own child's experience, but to all children in that school or program. Recent studies of what works to minimize bullying have found parental involvement and training to be one of the most beneficial.

This short assessment will allow you to reflect upon beliefs you may bring to the table when working with the program or school.

Questions for Parents		
N=No, Y=Yes, N/A= not applicable or no data		
Regarding your own experiences with bullying:		
1. When you were a child, did you have an adult you could go to?	N Y N/A	
2. When you were involved in bullying (in any role) did adults help?	N Y N/A	
Regarding the adults at your child's school/program:		
3. Can you approach them with bullying issues?	N Y N/A	
4. Do you trust them?	N Y N/A	
5. Are they helpful in resolving issues?	N Y N/A	
6. Are they willing to cooperate with you?	N Y N/A	

If you answered "no" to questions 1 and 2, be aware of how your own experience may affect your perspective or emotional response to your child's experience. You may feel mistrust of the school and question whether approaching them will make a difference for your child. Do your best to put your own experiences aside and to approach the school for your child's well- being. You may be pleasantly surprised and find some understanding and compassionate people.

If you answered "no" to questions 3, 4 or 5, have you taken any constructive steps to address your concerns? If you have taken steps and not seen any improvement, building a collaborative partnership with your child's school may not be possible. Reading this chapter may help you decide whether to approach the school or find another program.

What Does Not Work

Before launching into your options for changing your child's environment, it's worth a cautionary look at actions that generally are not helpful. How you approach the school and let them know that there is a way to stop bullying will be important in whether you are heard or just pushed aside as another "overprotective parent."

DON'T...	...because
Talk directly to the parents of the child who bullied yours	The other parents may see things differently and defend their child's behavior. This may lead to an increase in the bullying. Sometimes involving the other child's family is harmful to the other child, as bullying can be a family dynamic.
Fight all your child's battles	This is a reminder to leave room for other ways to address the problem besides adult intervention. You also want to empower your child with individual skills and strategies. Choose battles wisely.
Threaten to hire an attorney or start litigation	While these may be appropriate in rare cases, these will likely end collaboration with the school or program, and will not lead to any quick changes in your child's current situation.
Accuse the school of not being safe.	The school may become defensive, rather than collaborating to solve problems.
Complain and demand without offering to work together	Again, collaboration is the goal. Offer to be a part of the solution and the problem is more likely to get dealt with.

What Does Work

There are a number of actions that are more likely to be helpful in changing the climate, which primarily involve partnering with the school or program. Parents are a shaping force within a school or program. As a parent, you may be the first impetus for change and can be the one to spearhead improvements. Each classroom, on the average, has at least two children who are the victims of a bully. There are other concerned parents. You will not be alone if you make the effort to find them and involve them.

Calm Communication

The first thing to be said, and repeated, is that how you approach the school or program matters. Your attitude, tone, and initial approach are important in being heard and in developing a collaborative relationship. You must be in a calm frame of mind and be open to exploring a point of agreement. This does not mean that you may not have reasons to be angry: about events, about responses, about your child's safety. It does mean that you must find a way to return to a calm frame of mind before engaging with the school or program. Problem-solving, especially with others, requires thinking and conversation, as well as planning and collaboration. These activities are difficult to do well when one is flooded with emotion. One good test of whether you are in a calm frame of mind is whether you can talk normally. You need to be able to speak slowly, calmly, and with a normal tone and volume. Do not talk to anyone at the school until you can communicate about your child's experiences with a serious, focused, calm approach rather than a volatile, threatening, or highly emotional one.

The table on the next page provides tips on developing and maintaining a calm frame of mind.

Ways to Return to a Calm Frame of Mind	
Discharge Energy	Get rid of anger or pent up energy in a positive way. Anything from reasoned discussion with someone not directly involved, to making a plan, to exercising, to using breathing or relaxation techniques will work. What matters is finding a method that works for you.
Time	Waiting can do wonders. If you can determine that the situation is important, but that your immediate action isn't required, then waiting often helps. Maybe you can wait 24 hours. Maybe a couple hours. Even 15 minutes, especially if combined with another technique, such as exercising or breathing, may make a big difference.
Reframe	Remember that to change the climate at the school or program will require collaboration with those in that environment. Reframe them as your allies, not your enemies. Remember that your goal is to be on the same team. Reframe this as an opportunity to empower your community to help its children.

Approaching the School or Program

There are many ways for you to approach your child's school or program:

1. Start with one person only if you feel too angry or too intimidated by the school or community program as a whole. For example, talk to your child's teacher or coach and ask if he or she would like to work with you to form a partnership to explore ways to stop bullying. This may be a place to start before approaching the larger school or program community.

2. With the person(s) identified in the previous step, determine a point of agreement or some common ground. For example, can you and that point of contact agree that you both want a safe school environment?

57

3. Explore resources and inform the school or program of bullying-prevention or other programs for dealing with the problem. (See the Resource Guide at the end of this book.) Remember that fidelity to program implementation protocol is critical for program success.

4. Talk to other parents. Generate positive interest and support.

5. Join the Parent Teacher Association, or other parent group, and generate interest and support from them.

6. Make an appointment with the school principal, program leader, or appropriate counseling or mental health staff member. Express your concern without criticizing. Inform them that you would like to work together to create a safer environment not only for your child but for others as well. Offer yourself as an ally in solving the problem. Discuss how to make the climate safe and inclusive for all—physically, socially, and psychologically.

Once you have decided to share your concerns with a representative of the school or program, here is a structure to navigate the process of problem-solving.

Step 1: Initiate Collaboration

Meet with the teacher, coach, or leader to express your concern and share information about your child's vulnerabilities as well as temperament. This would be a time to discuss what you found as you gathered data in Part II, sharing concerns, asking questions or for clarification, and listening to responses. Assess whether this is an adult who is comfortable with social and emotional issues as well as capable of standing up to power dynamics and intervening. Ask, "Is this an ally?"

Step 2: ⮞ Develop a Plan Together

Together, create a plan for dealing with the issues you brought to the table. If possible, set dates and identify measureable or observable outcomes to help all parties follow up and determine if there has been change. Set a time frame in your mind of approximately four weeks.

Step 3: ⮞ Follow Up

Re-assess at that time whether you have seen follow-through and positive changes. If so, congratulate yourself on your positive use of your power, and continue to collaborate, set goals, and assess results. If no change is seen within four weeks, it is unlikely that this social environment will change. In this case, seriously consider whether your child needs to change schools or find a new activity or community program. This option is discussed at the end of this chapter.

Remember that:

- Having a bullying prevention program is no assurance that bullying does not exist. Some bullying prevention programs have not been demonstrated to be effective. Other bullying prevention programs are not fully implemented throughout the school. As new children enter the school and others leave, the power dynamics and climate shift.

- Not all teachers are comfortable with social and emotional issues. Some see that their job is to teach or to coach their area of expertise only and not to solve social problems.

- The difference between bullying and normal conflict is not something adults recognize unless educated on the topic. Some adults will think you are exaggerating, over-reacting, or over-protecting.

- Some bullies are "slick", engaging and well-liked by peers and adults. These children are very difficult to spot and the adult with whom you are discussing your child may not have witnessed any of the behaviors you are describing.

Final Thoughts

If you meet with resistance from the school or program in making positive changes:

- Consider if a change of school or program is needed, as detailed in the next section.

- Find out about local resources for child and family advocacy. These may exist through the public school system and other public or government agencies, or you may find a private advocate.

- Focus on your child's abilities and skills in the section "Empowering Your Child."

Chapter 8

When to Change Schools or Programs

As many as 20% of children say they are frightened through much of the school day. Many avoid the bathroom, lunchroom, and playground because these places are poorly supervised and are where most bullying occurs. Parents don't always know what or how much to believe of what they hear from their children. Too often, children do not tell anyone about their fears. They report that no one helps them anyway and they fear that the bully will retaliate. Parents are appalled when they hear this. They consider school to be a place where children can find help if they need it. Unfortunately, this is often not the case. Many schools have installed metal detectors and most schools have a weapons policy. Sadly, as we know from recent tragedies, these safeguards do not always work nor do they stop the fear and intimidation a bully instills. Teachers cannot be there at every moment and bullies can be clever. They can create a sense of fear in a matter of seconds without teachers or staff ever suspecting what is happening.

If a school or program is not capable of protecting your child, either through unwillingness to accept that there is a problem or to address it, the parent must act. The "red flags" list can help you decide.

> ### Red Flags
>
> 1. Your child has been targeted repeatedly and over a long period of time.
>
> 2. Your child is so frozen with fear that he or she cannot use the protective strategies.
>
> 3. Your child is high risk on the risk assessment scale.
>
> 4. Your child is expressing a strong sense of hopelessness and sadness.
>
> 5. Your child's behaviors have changed significantly without obvious known cause (i.e. acting sad, withdrawn, or engaging in risky behaviors).
>
> 6. Your child does not have a single friend in the current setting.
>
> 7. The school or program has been unresponsive to your concerns and has no focus on positive school climate.
>
> 8. The bullying has escalated to a dangerous level. The cruelty is so intense that your child is avoiding school, feeling very anxious, or physically sick.
>
> 9. As a parent, you have lost trust in the school and feel you have no collaborative relationships within the school.

Multiple schooling options are available today for parents to consider. These include:

- Public schools
- Charter schools
- Option schools
- Home schooling
- Virtual schools
- Independent private schools
- Religiously-based schools

When looking for a new school for your child, find one that has a school climate or bullying prevention program that focuses on changing bystanders to upstanders.

Charter schools with varying educational philosophies and cultural approaches exist in most major cities. In some school districts, parents can sign their children up at option schools which are alternative choices to their neighborhood school. Home schooling networks, materials and online support are expanding for parents who have the time and resources. Virtual or online academies are available from kindergarten through high school. Children schooled in any of these formats are just as competitive in gaining admission to college as those applying from traditional schools. In fact, children become better learners when the environment is safe and they are free of fear.

Most other programs, such as sports or music programs, are of a more optional nature than school. In any case, when considering an alternative school or program, use the tools in Part II to assess and gather data, and consider the fit for your child. The section entitled Building on Strengths will also be a good resource.

Chapter 9

Empowering Your Child

Just as there are things you can and can't (or shouldn't) do to change your child's environment, so too, there are things that can and can't (and shouldn't) be changed about your child. Focus on the areas that offer opportunities for growth for your child. In this section you will find skills and strategies that fit different temperaments and ages, so that you can tailor your plan. Select one or two skills or strategies to focus on at a time. If one doesn't work, come back to select another one. If a skill is mastered, choose another to add to your child's toolbox. This is an opportunity for character growth, and empowering your child in dealing with bullying and adversity. Picture these skills as a shield that your child can use to protect against bullies. The child can develop and use his or her own positive power, rather than give it away to the bully.

Think for a moment:

What are your child's triggers or buttons? (*These are the actions or comments others make that arouse a strong emotional response in your child.*)

✓ Find strategies that address these triggers.

What are your child's strengths? *Look back at the Temperament and Competencies Assessment in Part II, and also consider other more unique strengths, such as sense of humor.*

✓ Find strategies that build on these strengths.

What You Can't Change

Remember your child's vulnerabilities from your assessment in Part II. Many of the vulnerabilities that a bully may target are characteristics that cannot or should not be changed, such as height, skin color, ethnicity, abilities or disabilities, or interests. Some features may be changeable, such as hair color or clothing style; but a family may want to support their child in those differences. Some differences are a source of pride and identity, such as wearing a burqa, a yarmulke, long skirts, or other identifiers of race, culture, or family values. While the vulnerabilities themselves may not be changeable, sometimes it is how a child responds to targeting that makes all the difference. Empowering the child is the focus of the rest of this book.

What You Can Do

You can help your child build a toolbox of skills and strategies that will be useful in bullying and other difficult situations. Although you cannot change the natural disposition of your child, you can do a great deal to build and expand a child's competencies.

In Part II you assessed the risk factors for your child, both internal to the child, and in the environment or situation. This will inform your choice of strategies. You also need to look a little deeper at the type of reaction your child typically has: are they over-reactive, under-reactive, or flexible? This, too, will help you align strategies with your child's needs. You will assess reactivity first, and add this to your thinking as you select ways to empower your child.

The remainder of the book covers many ways to empower your child:
- Knowing When and How to Disengage
- Learning Protective Strategies
- Making Good Peer Choices
- Crushing Cyberbullying
- Building on Strengths
- Working with Resistant Children
- Shaping a Bystander into an Upstander

Recognizing Your Child's Reactive Style

Two types of victims were described earlier: passive victims and provocative victims. Passive victims are the ones who don't fight back or stick up for themselves. They give in because they lack the temperament and/or social skills to defend themselves physically and psychologically. After trying meekly, they hide out of fear and anxiety. These children may not be fun for others to play with so they end up alone or with few friends. Bullies find them easy to pick on because they don't know how to protect themselves. As you

look at the scale on the next page, passive victims fall toward the under-reactive end of the scale.

Provocative victims are at the opposite end of the same scale. These children are restless, thin-skinned and irritable, and will respond with noise or fuss, or will fight back, though often ineffectively. They may even provoke, tease, and "egg on" the bully, which can be mistakenly used to justify a bully's aggression. Yet they lose and usually end up ridiculed. When they lose, they, too, may have exaggerated and dejected body postures. Their problem is over-reactivity. They leap right into new experiences without thinking. They also wear parents to exhaustion with their activity level and "accident proneness." These children also often have few friends.

- The under-reactive child is at risk of becoming a passive victim.
- The over-reactive child is at risk of becoming a provocative victim.

Knowing your child and rating him or her along the continuum below will guide you in which behaviors need reshaping to avoid bullying. Rate your child's reactivity on the scale below:

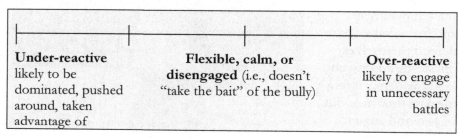

Under-reactive
likely to be
dominated, pushed
around, taken
advantage of

**Flexible, calm, or
disengaged** (i.e., doesn't
"take the bait" of the bully)

Over-reactive
likely to engage
in unnecessary
battles

Many parents are clear about which tendency their child exhibits. If you feel uncertain, complete the next assessment.

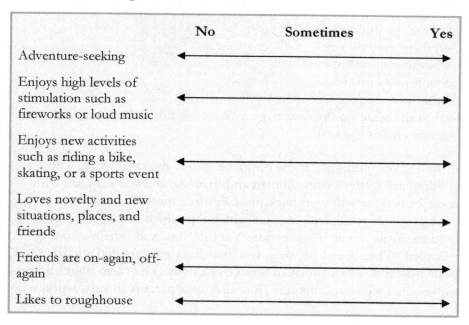

	No	Sometimes	Yes
Adventure-seeking	◄—————————————►		
Enjoys high levels of stimulation such as fireworks or loud music	◄—————————————►		
Enjoys new activities such as riding a bike, skating, or a sports event	◄—————————————►		
Loves novelty and new situations, places, and friends	◄—————————————►		
Friends are on-again, off-again	◄—————————————►		
Likes to roughhouse	◄—————————————►		

Look at where your checks are. If they are nearer to the right-hand side of the scale, you probably have an over-reactive or provocative child. If they are nearer to the left-hand side of the scale, your child is more likely to be under-reactive and at risk to be a passive victim. If your child is in the middle or "sometimes" column, he or she has a more flexible reaction style and is not as likely to be bullied. These children are resilient. They "roll with the punches" and shift gears as necessary.

Now that you have rated your child, you know if you have an under-reactive or over-reactive child. Life events and circumstances may also further shape or entrench a child's basic disposition. These external events may not be something you can prevent or change. Although you cannot change the natural disposition of your child, a parent can do a great deal to shape a child's reactivity. However, you will benefit your child by helping shape his or her behaviors away from the extremes.

The following tables offer some general guidelines:

Under-reactive children benefit from:
• Modeling and encouragement to express feelings.
• Social skills training—what to say and how to say it.
• Gradual exposure to new experiences.
• Learning skills to manage anxiety.
• Support—but not over-protectiveness — during difficult times to help meet the challenges.
• Being allowed to experience some of life's difficulties and hard moments.
• Building on strengths.

Over-reactive children benefit from:

- Learning to express emotions, especially anger, in a regulated manner.
- Learning self-regulation skills—for example "stop and think."
- Understanding cause and effect.
- Clearly and firmly point out the consequences of their own actions
- Earning freedom and privileges.
- Guidance and discussion rather than punishment without explanation.
- Direction and help in learning specific skills for getting their needs met appropriately.
- Rehearsing scripted strategies.
- Learning to see themselves as others see them.
- Being expected to have compassion and empathy for others.
- Being expected to do thoughtful things for others.
- Participating in cooperative group activities.

Knowing When and How to Disengage

Your child must first learn what to ignore, what to respond to, and when to walk away. If a child chooses to respond, the best response is assertive (neither too aggressive nor too passive), brief, and followed by walking away. Sometimes walking away is not possible, given circumstances, but emotional disengagement is possible. Not "taking the bait" is a valuable skill to learn. Over and under-reactive children may need special coaching to get this right. These skills are taught in this chapter.

Step 1:   Evaluate the Situation

Encourage your child, when faced by a bully, to think first. Assess the advantages of both taking a stand and walking away. Decide if this is a battle worth fighting. Teach your child to choose when to engage, and to have the skills to be able to choose to walk away or disengage. The use of the specific strategies in combination with disengagement is a very powerful tool.

Many problems are solved just by walking away and controlling emotion. It takes two to fight, and choosing to leave a fight is sometimes the best strategy. It may come as a surprise to learn this is the most difficult strategy for children to learn. Most children want to fight back or to get the last word in. They think that if they walk away, they have not won. Even shy children who walk away tend to do it without assertiveness and determination. Choosing not to fight does not mean meekly giving in. It means taking away the bully's power by refusing to engage with him or her. The bully wants a reaction. Bullies feel powerful when they see the pain and suffering of the victim. By not becoming emotional, not showing pain and suffering, but rather by walking away in an assertive manner, the bully's bluff has been called. When the child takes a stand, this too is a brief and assertive action followed by disengagement, leaving the bully with no one to fight. These are strategies you can practice with your child. Choosing not to fight can be a winning strategy when the target effectively takes control. The biggest winners are those who are not on the scene when violence escalates.

The following table lists some general guidelines you can use to teach your child when to take a stand and when to choose to let it go.

General Tips for Evaluating a Situation

Take a stand if...	Let it go if...
There are threats of physical or sexual assault	The threats are more pat phrases, idioms, or figures of speech than real threats
There are strong derogatory remarks about race, ethnicity, or family that are constant, intense, or repetitive	There are occasional racial remarks or ethnic put-downs that are primarily insensitive, not cruel. Education may be a better remedy than escalation.
There is extortion of large amounts of money	Small amounts of money are demanded and there is no giving back
This is a relationship that is important and/or there is caring for the other person	There is no relationship and no interest in building one
A bully shows some capacity for compassion, empathy, and mutuality	It is a child who can both give and take. Offer once to share, state what you expect in return, and see what happens.
Bullying behavior is increasing in magnitude and intensity	Bullying behavior is constant, but there are no signs of escalation

Step 2: Decide When and How to Disengage

The situation is one factor in determining whether to first take a stand, or simply to let it go. Another factor is your child's temperament. Depending on the age of your child, you may want to review their reactive tendency together. Look at the line below. (It is the same line you saw on page 68.)

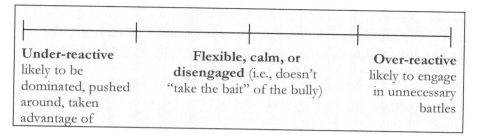

Under-reactive	Flexible, calm, or	Over-reactive
likely to be	disengaged (i.e., doesn't	likely to engage
dominated, pushed	"take the bait" of the bully)	in unnecessary
around, taken		battles
advantage of		

Where did your child fall on the line? When choosing among the skills and strategies that follow, work on those that match your child's temperament. Keep in mind that the most effective, and often the easiest skill to master, is disengagement or "don't take the bait." Remember that bullies enjoy power as well as the spotlight. When they cannot gain these, they may not reform, but will typically find a different target.

Step 3: Move Toward the Middle

The ultimate goal is for your child to build skills that shape toward the middle. Effective children size up a situation and decide quickly what to do, pulling from a toolbox of skill and strategy choices. They are not bound by their tendency to be over-reactive or under-reactive. They have the personal strength to make a conscious choice. They also have the skills to put their choice into action.

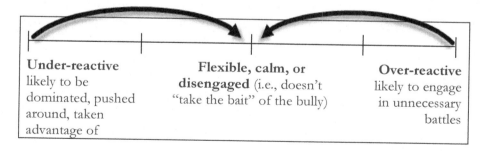

Under-reactive	Flexible, calm, or	Over-reactive
likely to be	disengaged (i.e., doesn't	likely to engage
dominated, pushed	"take the bait" of the bully)	in unnecessary
around, taken		battles
advantage of		

If you have an under-reactive child, your goal is to teach how not to be taken advantage of, and avoid being a passive victim. If you have an over-reactive child, your goal is to teach what is worth reacting to and not to fight back against every provocation, thus avoiding being a provocative victim. Children who are targeted but do not become victims don't over-do and don't under-do.

Learning to disengage effectively and not react to every slight, taunt, threat, or put-down is one of the most important skills you can teach your child. Disengagement means making an assertive statement with self-confidence (or ignoring) and then walking away with a confident manner. A child who says nothing and slinks away, eyes on the ground and shoulders slumped, is not skilled at disengagement. The bully takes one look and knows he or she has won. The body language says, "I'm terrified and too afraid to say or do anything." Similarly, a child who stays to trade taunts and put downs, or looks angry and upset has played right into the bully's hands.

A child must practice the walk, the style, and the presentation of disengagement. Take a stand, say a few simple words, shoulders up, head high, and then turn and walk away, maintaining a positive and confident body posture.

Disengaging: Including Hints for Over- or Under-reactive Children

Following are the basic steps to disengaging, for all children. If your child is under-reactive, assertive engagement, such as speaking up, will be harder. Remind your child that bullies like having power over passive victims. If your child is over-reactive, the withdrawal and walking away will be the most difficult. Remind your child that bullies like power struggles, so if your child engages in a struggle, the bully wins. Do role plays with your child, so he or she can practice appropriate responses. Bullies are not likely to change or stop the first time your child responds in a new manner. Bullies will "come back for seconds" again and again. It will take time and perseverance.

1. Take a Stand (Or Not)

If a situation calls for taking a stand, make a brief, clear statement that is not open-ended and not emotional. Indicate that you intend to ignore what was said or done. Know that this is a quick step.

- Tip for the under-reactive child: Taking a stand can help you feel in control. Use positive body posture and a normal indoor voice. Making eye contact will make your response stronger. For example: "You are welcome to your opinion," or "I'll share this time; it will be your turn next time."

- Tips for the over-reactive child: Think twice - see if you can skip this and just let it go. If you do take a stand - it is brief and unemotional. Use a normal indoor voice, calm your body posture. Example: "I don't get into fights over things like this," or "I'm proud of who I am."

2. Let it Go

Disengage and leave if possible. Walk away with positive body posture: head high, shoulders straight, decisively; aim yourself towards someone (Step 4). Distract yourself with other thoughts such as mathematics (counting down from 10 or 100, multiplication, doubling), listing all the things you are good at, or thinking about your favorite things or places.

- Tip for the under-reactive child: Look confident, act confident, and your feelings will follow (or at least not show!) If you can't walk away, maintain positive body posture. Move quickly to the next step.

- Tips for the over-reactive child: Remember to move at a normal pace, steady, and with a calm body. If you can't walk away, continue with lots of self-distraction and positive self-talk. Try not to make eye contact with the aggressors; try to ignore.

3. Think Useful Thoughts

Do not continue to think about what the other person said or did. Do not give the bully that control in your mind. Instead, use positive self-talk (out loud for younger, in the mind for older children), and continue to distract yourself from dwelling on the incident.

- <u>Tip for the under-reactive child</u>: Remember your family, friends, pets, — others who care about you. Ex: "That person's opinions don't matter to me. I am confident of my own." Ex: "I won't let that person upset me."

- <u>Tips for the over-reactive child</u>: Winning is not who is best at put-downs. Not responding means I win — I didn't give them a show. Ex: "I'm in control of my emotions." Ex: "Back to work/play!"

4. Go Towards Others

Don't just walk away, walk toward a teacher, friend, parent, or other accepting social situation. Get involved in something more positive and good for you!

5. Talk to Someone

Talk to a trusted person to get another perspective on what happened. See if the trusted person thought that what was said was intentionally hurtful or upsetting. Sometimes we are hurt or upset about things that were not intentional.

- <u>Tip for the under-reactive child</u>: Sometimes we feel more hurt because we did not take a stand for ourselves.

- <u>Tips for the over-reactive child</u>: Sometimes we fight battles where it wasn't necessary.

6. Make a Plan

This is also a proactive step – having a plan makes the target feel more in control of the situation. Remember that the bully often will try again – but you will be ready.

- Tip for the under-reactive child: Practice taking a stand, the words you could use, and an assertive tone. Use a mirror to practice posture and watch others to see how to look confident.

- Tips for the over-reactive child: Have someone role-play trying to upset you, as you practice the disengaging steps. Identify triggers and practice your skills against those.

Chapter 10

Learning Protective Strategies

All children need to feel confident in their ability to protect themselves when picked on. Select strategies to fit your child's temperament and reactivity, and to address specific situations they may have encountered. These will serve as a protective shield against aggression and bullying.

These protective strategies are from the Bully-Proofing Your School program, which your child's school may be using. These strategies help the targeted child to stay unemotional, choose how to respond, disengage, and leave the situation. All are effective and easy to use. All children can learn them. When you feel scared, it's difficult to think. The simple names for the strategies are designed to be memorable under stress.

For *young children* the strategy for dealing with a bully is: **"Talk, Walk and Go for Help"**

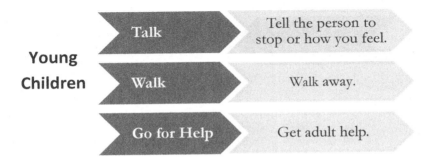

Young Children	Talk	Tell the person to stop or how you feel.
	Walk	Walk away.
	Go for Help	Get adult help.

For *school-aged children* the strategy for dealing with a bully is: **"HA HA SO"**.

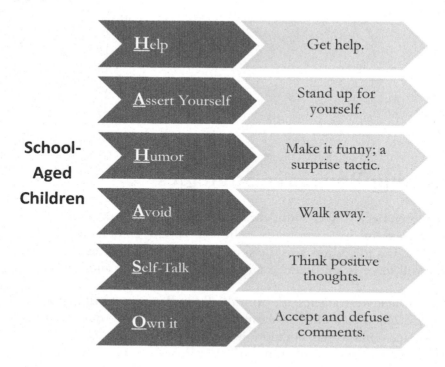

School-Aged Children

Help	Get help.
Assert Yourself	Stand up for yourself.
Humor	Make it funny; a surprise tactic.
Avoid	Walk away.
Self-Talk	Think positive thoughts.
Own it	Accept and defuse comments.

For *teenagers* the strategy for dealing with a bully is: **"HA HA SORT"**. It is the same as the school-aged strategy, plus:

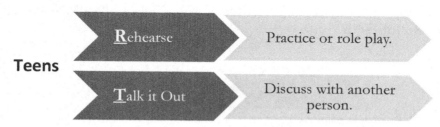

Teens

Rehearse	Practice or role play.
Talk it Out	Discuss with another person.

The following list provides additional details on the terminology included in the bully-proofing strategies.

Help means knowing *when* and *how* to get assistance from others. It also means knowing *who* can help. Talk to your child about who the adults and children are who can be counted on for support.

Assert Yourself means learning when to stand up to a bully and when not to. To use this strategy, the target looks the bully in the eye and says, "I don't like you telling untrue stories about me. What you are doing is mean. Stop doing it." This strategy should not be used in instances of severe bullying or when the target could be injured.

Humor means turning a difficult situation into a funny one. This is a surprise tactic, which usually catches the bully off guard. Other kids will laugh and the bully gets defused. This is a difficult strategy for a frightened child. Thinking on your feet, especially thinking of something funny, is not easy when you feel afraid. Getting ideas from stories, parents, movies, and any other source can help. Practicing good comebacks also helps. Don't use tactics that put down the bully because this will make matters worse. The idea is to change the situation from a power play to a funny situation.

Avoid means knowing how and when to walk away. This is the strategy most children use. Some go to enormous lengths to avoid running into the bully. Disengagement is one form of avoidance, but a more difficult one than just staying out of the bully's reach. Disengagement is walking away while leaving an assertive message that you are not interested in engaging in conflict. It takes courage and practice, but it is well worth it.

Self Talk is a way to continue to feel good about yourself when someone else is putting you down. Children can imagine playing a CD or audio clip in their heads that contains good thoughts and positive messages. You can help your child by working to develop these positive statements.

Own It means agreeing with the put-down in order to make light of it. It means developing the capacity to laugh at oneself. This strategy is easy to use and very effective because the bully does not expect it. It is best used when being teased or made fun of about something such as clothing or hairstyle. "I agree with you. This shirt is the ugliest color I've ever seen. Glad you think so too," might be an "own it" comeback. If, on the other hand, your child is being put down about something inherent to his identity or person, such as ethnicity, religion, or disability, this tactic is not a good idea because it could lower his self-esteem.

Rehearse is practicing a response or comeback. Some children think on their feet easily while others literally freeze when confronted with a cruel remark or behavior. Parents can create practice scenarios and work on responses that their children are capable of delivering. Humor is the most difficult while owning the put down (provided it is not about your child's identity) is one of the easiest as it defuses the power dynamic

Talk it Out is especially important for the quick-to-react or overly sensitive child. This means sharing a situation with a trusted adult who will listen empathically, offer reassurance that the put down was not deserved, and will provide some space and time for calming down and reflecting.

Learning the right strategy for the situation takes time and practice. Sometimes the first thing tried does not work. This is why there are a number of strategies and easy acronyms to remember them. Help your child use his or her protective shield by practicing each strategy. Just like a pilot practices emergency procedures, children also must practice to be ready for a real "emergency" or bully situation. Like a pilot, your child will think more clearly and react with his or her best effort if there have been practice sessions.

Making Good Peer Choices

Children's friends can also be their enemies. It is not always easy to tell when the boundary has been crossed. One simple rule is that a friendship has evolved into bullying when one of the children is taking far more than he or she is giving. Yet, some children enjoy and benefit from bossy or take-charge friends. What, then, can help a parent to know when a friendship has turned toward a bullying relationship?

Parents may not be able to directly influence the friends their children select to be with at school or in activities, but they can listen, talk about their concerns, and build good judgment. Friendships change over time and across situations. Children may need guidance to understand that friendship is a give-and-take relationship. Repeated mistreatment

> *Recall that bullying occurs when there is **no benefit to the victim**. Bullying is a **one-sided** relationship in which the victim is exploited and used.*

is not friendship. Children often need help in recognizing this, defining healthy limits, working toward change, and even ending a relationship if improvement is not possible. Sometimes a "vacation" from a friendship can help a child to see things more clearly. Evaluating the relationship along the following positive and negative dimensions can provide a more complete picture for making decisions.

If only one or possibly two negative dimensions are present, you may want to encourage your child to work toward improvement in these areas only. If, on the other hand, many of these dimensions are present, the friendship may not be a friendship at all but a bullying relationship.

Let's look individually at the negative dimensions.

1. There is no empathy, responsiveness, or problem-solving.

Problem-solving is learned gradually in the middle years of childhood. Not until age eight or nine do most children recognize the concept of "fairness" and how to talk through difficulties. To have the capacity to problem-solve, a child must first be able to recognize another child's needs. This involves awareness of others, the capacity to listen and process feelings, and some appreciation that each person is unique in what hurts feelings. A self-serving child is one who always places his or her needs above all other considerations. Even if your child and his or her friend cannot problem-solve together, watch to see if one or both can accept a fair solution when you offer it. If fairness is repeatedly turned down and only a self-serving outcome is acceptable, then the friendship has turned toward becoming a bullying relationship. This type of interactional style – with limited willingness to problem solve or understand the other's point of view – is a poor prognosis for shaping a balanced and satisfying relationship.

2. There is repeated maltreatment over time and situations.

Some children are forced into social settings that are small and in which they are not comfortable. These children have no choice in selecting friends. They are "stuck" in a small environment of peers, be that at school, on the bus, in the neighborhood, at church, or in an activity group. They are essentially captive. They don't have the choice to walk away and find another group of peers to join.

Negativity in small settings often starts with ostracism—being picked on for being different, not being included, or being pushed outside of a group by established cliques. Children want to be included socially. One child can be singled out to be excluded, and all of the other children become invested in keeping this child in the underdog role. Changing roles is very difficult once a child has been placed at the bottom of the social-acceptance ladder. This situation often starts with just one child making a cruel remark. This gets the ball rolling and others quickly join in order to affirm their own status in the peer group. As these children don't want to lose their position, they actively join in bullying the target. Others may remain passive, looking on but allowing the mistreatment to occur. Over time the situation can escalate into one of extreme hurtfulness and viciousness.

Group rejection can become almost mob-like. When asked, other children will often justify joining in the cruelty by saying that everyone else does it and that makes it okay. Wanting to be accepted by the group is a powerful influence for many children.

3. The relationship changes to one of maltreatment when peers are present.

Some friendships seem to change dramatically when other children are present. Your child may play successfully with a peer one-on-one, only to find that he or she is treated very differently in the presence of peers. These are "underground friendships" because they exist away from the eyes of the rest of the world. As a parent, you need to understand these relationships before planning what to do. Typically, the child who changes loyalties in this way does it to find acceptance in the peer group. He or she is unlikely to be the ringleader of the bullying behavior; rather, this is a child who plays by the rules the bully sets when the bully is present, but is more of his or her own person when alone.

4. There is an element of cruelty.

Some children are clueless and truly lack any awareness of how their negative behavior feels to others. This may be due to deprivation in learning this awareness, but help is available and effective in improving children's social skills. Other children in this category actually get pleasure out of hurting others. They may be hard-core, angry children who don't want help and will not accept it. This type of child is not one you can turn into a friend by any means. These children are determined to win and they will become more vicious in order to "get even" or "be one up". Teach your child to stay away from these children. They will never become friends.

Some children are frightening. They will hurt others and many grow up to be criminals who feel pleasure in watching others suffer. This is way beyond what any child should be handling. Authority figures must be brought in to help with situations this serious and intense. No child, whether target or bystander, has the capacity to cope with this level of cruelty. Don't try to rectify the situation.

5. There is no mutuality.

Remember that in the give-and-take of friendship, there can be periods of neediness in which one child gives more and the other needs more. Ups and downs are normal, but there must be something in the history of the relationship that promises the give-and-take will be restored in the future. Otherwise, the relationship becomes one-sided.

What can the family do?

The following list gives a concise summary of what you can do to help your child. Use discussion and role play, as appropriate.

1. Help your child evaluate his or her friendships along the five dimensions. Gently advise your child to get out of a friendship if too many dimensions are worrisome.

2. Balance the odds for your child by building resiliency and social skills.

3. Mobilize the community to change the climate and make it safer for all.

4. Contact an authority figure who will work with you in a confidential manner if you believe your child is being bullied by a seriously cruel and sadistic child.

5. Do not contact the parents of the bully on your own. Parents of bullies often defend their own bully and the problem can get worse, not better. Use your connections in the community to bring about change by mobilizing institutions into action.

6. Talk with your child to identify who the helpful adults are. Not all adults are helpful. Children constantly report that they went to a person whose title or position indicated the adult would help only to be told, "You are old enough to solve your own problems." Ask your child, "Who do you think would help you?" Let your child name some people. You may be surprised at your child's awareness and resourcefulness.

7. Remember that children drift in and out of friendships. Do not attempt to repair some friendships or encourage friends who have lost their appeal. Some change is inevitable as different ages bring new interests, activities, and possibilities for friendship. Few children keep their childhood friends for life.

Part IV:

Special Applications

- Dealing with Cyberbullying
- Building on Strengths
- Working with Children with Special Needs
- Working with Resistant Children
- What if Your Child Is The Bully? Developing Positive Power
- Shaping a Bystander into an Upstander

Chapter 11

Dealing with Cyberbullying

Cyberbullying includes the sending of humiliating, derogatory or threatening emails or text messages; postings on websites or in chat rooms; or forwarding confidential emails. It is basically old-fashioned bullying, just enacted within the new virtual world our children

increasingly inhabit. Cyberbullying has some unique characteristics: greater anonymity of the bully, no physical or time-limited boundary, and a potentially vast public audience. While there are ways to  track down cyberbullies, the bully's feeling of anonymity can lead to more vicious bullying than if the encounter were face-to-face. Similarly, the target may feel even greater emotion in the face of unknown and seemingly unstoppable assailants and a potentially unlimited audience. And, unlike face-to-face bullying, it can take place 24/7 via phones and computers, leaving little respite for the target.

If you have established open communication with your child, and take preventive measures, you have a better chance of knowing if he or she is being bullied online. In this section you will also find resources and strategies to take action if cyberbullying occurs.

Preventive Measures

Parents must establish boundaries and rules for online communications just as they do for other aspects of daily life. Ideas for instituting safe online behaviors include:

- Explicitly identify cyberbullying as bullying - just in a different "place" and treat it as such.

- Discuss how to respond to cyber aggression, including when to tell an adult.

- Use filtering and software programs that block specific content — on all electronic devices. You may be surprised how many devices allow an internet connection!

- Monitor your child's online activities, with their full awareness of this. Gradually grant increased freedom as it is earned.

- Provide clear rules and expectations for online behaviors, verbally, or in written contracts. (Examples of behaviors you might want to promote: Having your child seek permission to download any applications or files; or having your child seek permission before sharing private information such as an address or phone number.)

- Educate your child about how easily and quickly cyberbullying can create pain for others.

- Model and teach empathy, morals and values, including the value of face-to-face communication.

- Be aware of current laws, and convey to your child (age-appropriately) that some acts have permanent or long-term repercussions affecting one's record.

- Be aware of the permanency of electronic data and impacts on future school or job applications.

Responding to Cyberbullying

When cyberbullying happens, take action.

1. **If the cyberbullying took place at school or was initiated by other students, contact the school.** Many schools refuse to take responsibility for cyberbullying that occurs off the school premises even though students at the school were likely perpetrators. If the school's technology devices were used to perpetrate the bullying, the school will be more willing to be involved. Often this violation of technology use is covered in the school's code of conduct that students sign. Also, schools often have a technology curriculum, which includes safe use of technology. Parents may be able to collaborate with the school regarding this curriculum.

2. **Distance your child from the threat.** Find a way to stop the incoming threats. This may involve changing email addresses, phone numbers, and logins to sites. Discuss who to share any new addresses with. While it may help to keep the child off the internet as a first line of defense, children will feel isolated and punished if their freedom is restricted unduly as a response to someone else's wrong-doing. Continue to pursue justice, but also freedom for your child in a safe online environment.

3. **Save evidence.** Save emails, texts, or whatever you can as documentation of the cyberbullying.

4. **Report the threat.** If the threat took place on a social internet site, contact the provider to see about alternatives such as removing a site, a post, or barring an individual from further posts (i.e. if they

did not follow site rules; note that they may try again under a different alias). If remedies are not found through the above means, and the bullying is severe or continues, contact your local police department.

Increasingly, tools are being developed, books written and legal mandates passed to address cyberbullying. Look in the Additional Resources section at the end of this book to find these.

Chapter 12

Building on Strengths

Pursuing a child's strengths, interests and talents builds self-confidence, friendships, and social interactional skills. These are often outside of school activities through community centers, private organizations or parent groups. Often parents choose sports without considering whether the sport itself or the team is a match that will build on positives for their child. Below is a discussion of points to consider in assessing sports programs, and other programs that build on a child's talents, interests, and aptitudes.

Participation in Sports

Sports have a culture of their own. While parents hope that participating in sports will build sportsmanship, skills, and friendships, it is also the case that power, size, and skill are often important elements of winning. Unfortunately, winning can sometimes become more important than sportsmanship. Rivalry with other teams can become intense. Ethnic differences may get highlighted to an undesirable extent, and parents often extend their own unfulfilled dreams to their children.

Some children withstand these issues. Those who do are likely to be physically suited to the sport and mature enough to handle the pressure to succeed. For the child who lacks physical stature, ability, or emotional maturity, team sports can be brutally humiliating. It is notable that seventy percent of all children drop out of organized sports between ages 8 to 13.

Assessing Whether Your Child Is Suited to Team Sports

Parents need to consider the climate of a sports team or recreational activity when selecting one for their child. Many times a sport is selected because it is high profile in the culture, it has significance to the parent, it is held at a convenient time or place, or the child's best friend is participating in it. Parents would be wise to think about their child's skill and maturity, and to watch to see the level of competitiveness. Neighborhood recreational teams are often preferable to high-pressure competitive leagues, especially for children under the age of 13.

Before enrolling your child in a sport, do the following:

1. Assess your child for:
    - Interest level
    - Skill
    - Capacity to handle competition
    - Reactivity style (under-reactive, over-reactive, flexible)
    - Stamina
    - Emotional maturity

2. Observe the coach's style and a team practice:
    - What is the program's stated mission? Is it positive, inclusive and educational? Is it recreational or highly competitive?
    - Does it sound like your child will have fun and learn something?
    - Is there training for the coaches within a philosophy based on positive coaching strategies?
    - Is there supervision and evaluation of the coaches?
    - What is the expectation regarding parent involvement? (It is preferable to have parents "at arm's length".)
    - Is there a standard time all youth get to play/participate?
    - Is instruction at a level the children can understand?

3. Watch the children on the team and talk with other parents:
    - Do parents and youth in the community report that the program is fun?
    - Are there team expectations regarding attendance at games and practices?
    - Are there team expectations regarding behavior of youth and parents?
    - How is sportsmanship supported and taught?
    - Is everyone included?

Now consider, as a parent, what you want your child to gain from participation. Think back for a moment on your experiences of success as well as your experiences of disappointment or failure. Are you possibly encouraging your child to fulfill your dreams—either the ones at which you succeeded or the ones you wish you had? Remember that very, very few people make a living playing sports. The goal is team building and fun.

Think about your child now:

- Is your child more suited to a team sport or an individual sport?
- Is your child more suited to a competitive sport or a recreational one?
- Who has the primary interest in the sport—you or your child?

Matching Your Child to a Sport

The child who will succeed at sports has the following characteristics:

- High energy
- Stamina
- Coordination
- Likes to set goals or be challenged
- Competitiveness
- Above average size, strength, or agility
- Good frustration tolerance
- Maturity
- Capacity to control anger
- Interpersonal skills
- Capacity to work with others in a group
- Likes to join

If your child has a deficit in skill or size, give serious consideration to skipping the mainstream sports. Look at areas such as track and field, skiing, fencing, and so on. These take skill but only require short bursts of focused attention. Size is not a serious part of success and some immaturity can be tolerated.

If your child has a deficit in social maturity, he or she is likely to frustrate quickly, to withdraw, to have temper outbursts, or to have difficulty sustaining attention. Look at individual sports such as karate, golf, bicycling, swimming, skateboarding, gymnastics or dance, or one-on-one sports such as tennis, racquetball, wrestling, martial arts, or boxing. Keep in mind that many individual sports still have a team culture.

Every child needs a recreational outlet. As a parent, help guide your child into one that will provide success and fun. High-glory sports are not the only activities out there. The most important thing is for your child to have fun.

Participating in Other Activities

Many children find a far more rewarding match to their temperament, interests and skills by pursuing cultural or other interests. A rich array of enriching programs exists. Take the time to explore your local resources and find one that will build on positives for your child, referring back to Part II for assessment tools to evaluate programs as needed.

Here are some types of activities you may find available through schools, churches, recreational, cultural, or governmental groups:

- Theater
- Improv/Comedy
- Music
- Art
- Dance
- Technology
- Gaming
- Science
- Chess
- Writing
- Film-making
- Environmental Learning
- Fishing
- Boys and Girls Clubs
- Crafting
- Learning Projects (i.e. 4H)
- Service Projects (such as through churches and charities)
- Language Learning
- Exchange Programs

Be creative and responsive to your child's interests! Perhaps your child has a dog and wants to try obedience training. Perhaps there is a poetry club at a local library. There are even online communities that may be appropriate (see the section on Dealing with Cyberbullying). What is important is for your child to have an opportunity to experience successes socially and in areas of ability. Your child may find friends who share similar interests and will develop confidence when his or her abilities can shine. Again, the goal is to have fun, while being engaged and involved positively with peers.

Chapter 13

Working with Children with Special Needs

Children with special needs are not only more likely to be targeted for bullying but if they have difficulty with emotional regulation, they also may be more likely to bully. Many have a visible stigma that makes them easy targets. Parents are often anxious and worried. Most notify the school and some make a point of educating the staff and other parents through a mailing or a presentation at the beginning of the school year. These students can become more empowered through the strategies, but will still need vigilant support from adults, and some have specific legal rights and recourse. (For example, they might be eligible for a 504 plan or an individualized education plan.)

Grouping these children together is unfair as they are unique with special issues that cross multiple domains. Some have health related issues that make them vulnerable to taunting, social isolation, and harassment. These can range from attention deficit disorder, migraines, seizures, asthma, alopecia, and, increasingly, food allergies.

Allergies

There is a fine line to walk in keeping a child with, say, a severe peanut allergy safe while still allowing them to interact at the lunch table, enjoy treats at school and stand up for themselves. Many schools have restricted peanuts from being served within the school; others will make accommodations if notified. Parents must intervene and educate the school beyond just the school nurse. All of the staff, teachers, coaches, administrators and especially lunch room personnel should be informed of allergens.

Physical Disabilities

Physical disabilities can range from visual and auditory challenges to being wheel chair bound or using assisted devices. Children with motor coordination problems are often singled out for bullying because of their gait, difficulty interacting on the playground, and social isolation. Many report having no friends or social support and that other kids imitate their disability.

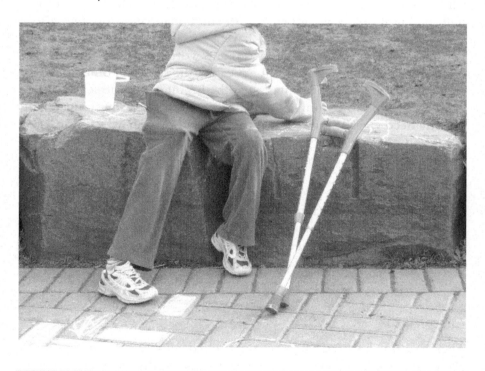

Emotional or Behavioral Challenges

Students with emotional/behavioral challenges, or conduct problems may lack impulse control and/or social awareness resulting in either being bullied, or in bullying others. Many students with these difficulties have individualized educational plans (IEPs), which are based on an assessment of a child's needs and designed in collaboration with a child's family.

Invisible Disabilities

Invisible disabilities may include learning differences, hidden physical health issues, or psychological challenges such as loss, trauma, or abuse. Many children and parents do not want to alert, much less even discuss, some hidden disabilities with the school. Some feel such issues are confidential and private to their family and others have experienced insensitive teachers, staff and other students. Primarily schools need to create a climate of inclusion for children with diverse backgrounds, families, needs and learning styles. Parents can work with schools or programs to improve climate, or be active in selecting programs with positive climates.

Gifted and Talented

Gifted children are often teased, ridiculed and harassed, with other students resenting the apparent ease with which they excel. Yet children who are cognitively advanced may not be equally advanced socially, emotionally or physically. They are sensitive and self-critical. Their coping strategies often include striking back with mean words or hiding their abilities. Sadly, these children sacrifice their cognitive strengths for the assurance of not being verbally bullied. All children deserve the assurance and comfort of knowing that they can be who they are within their school as long as they are not violating the rights of others to enjoy the same benefits.

Conclusion

If you suspect a problem:

- Make it a habit to talk to your child about school. Encourage your child to talk about his or her school day, friends, and worries or concerns.

- Find out who is involved in bullying, where it is happening and whether other students or adults are responsive.

- Keep a record of bullying described by your child.

- Inform yourself about school policies as well as state policies. Bullying legislation is in most states today. There is, however, no federal law that addresses bullying. Harassment laws are in place if a student is in a protected class which includes race, color, national origin, sex, religion and disabilities. A list of bullying laws can be found at: www.stopbullying.gov/laws/index.html or at www.cyberbullying.us.

- Inquire if your child's school has a code of conduct around cyberbullying. Some states have laws around electronic harassment. Work with your child's school to develop policies around both in school and out of school bullying via electronic means.

- Save emails, texts, or whatever you can as documentation of cyberbullying. If the threat took place on a social internet site, contact the provider to see about alternatives such as removing a site, a post, or barring an individual from further posts.

Chapter 14

Working with Resistant Children

Teaching your child to handle bullying problems is giving him or her skills for life. The ideas will be useful in many other difficult situations. You cannot be there at every moment. Involve your children in solving their own struggles. Teach them to think and trust that they can make their own good judgment calls.

Throughout this section, ideas have been presented for managing bullies. Some children, however, complain but resist help. They want you to do it for them. You may be tempted, but do not give in. A "Bully Intervention Plan" must involve your child in solving his or her problem. If you do it all yourself, then you, not your child, will learn and master the skills or strategies. Be cautious. Do not jump in too quickly with a solution. Allow your child to struggle a bit to create ideas. Make time for talking and problem-solving together.

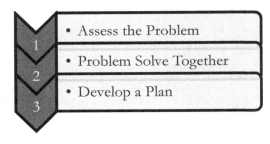

Roadblocks

Now, think for a moment about your child's style. As eager as most children are for relief from bullies, they typically want the adults to figure out a plan and take care of the problem for them. Talking about the bullying situation and creating a plan is not easy.

Children have an array of avoidance styles, or "roadblocks", that they use. Some of these are:

- *Whining about the problem but not solving it.* "You talk to him, Dad."

- *Refusing to talk.* "Butt out, Mom."

- *Blaming.* "It's the other guy's fault."

- *Giving up.* "There's nothing anyone can do that will help."

These tactics will probably distract you. They may cause you to feel that

the problem is too big to solve, that your child doesn't need or want any help, or, conversely, that only you are capable of solving the problem. It can be difficult to avoid getting stalled by your child's roadblocks and be taken in by his or her difficulty in facing a troublesome issue. You don't need to let that happen. Don't give in to helplessness, blaming, silence, or whining. Use the strategies that follow to assist you.

ACTIVITY

There are five questions you will want to explore as part of the dialogue and problem-solving discussion you have with your child. Think of it as an interview. Don't give the answers. If you were interviewing someone for a job, you wouldn't answer the questions for that person. If you did, you would never learn what the person was like and whether he or she had the skills for the job. This is precisely what you want to know about your own child. How was the problem experienced—did it create fear, anger, anxiety, or sadness? Does your child have appropriate ideas, skills, and solutions for handling it, or do some need to be suggested or created?

Ask these five questions. Be as objective as you can.
1. What happened?
2. How did you feel when this happened?
3. What part can you solve yourself?
4. What is the risk in doing this?
5. If this worked, what would be different?

Let's look now at the different styles children have when a parent attempts to get a dialogue started. Each style requires different methods of overcoming the resistance.

For the Reluctant Whiner

Try these strategies for the child who whines about the problem, rather than participates in planning and taking action.

1. Ask your child to list all of the barriers that get in the way of addressing a problem.

    a) Write them down. There may be as many as ten or more.

b) Don't react emotionally or say how silly certain complaints are; just listen and write.

c) Don't comment on your child's sense of helplessness.

2. Ask your child to put a star by the two he or she might be able to do something about.

3. Create a plan for these two areas. (Ignore the others for now).

Children who adopt this style truly feel overwhelmed with emotion and cannot move from the state of experiencing the feeling to creating a solution. They quickly flood with feelings, focus only on their own internal state, and panic at the thought that they might have to assert themselves to solve the problem. Often they have had others who problem solved for them in the past. They have learned to feel helpless and dependent rather than powerful and resourceful. No matter how small the effort they are willing to make, they will gain confidence from doing something rather than doing nothing.

Even if your child's plan is minuscule and you know it is not going to really solve the whole problem, encourage him or her and offer praise for having made a valiant effort. Encourage your child to use a friend, the peer group, or another helpful adult. If parents implement all of the aspects of the intervention plan, the child will not build confidence and strength. These children will benefit by exerting themselves to struggle to the extent that they are capable.

For the Silent Sufferer

Try these strategies for the child who won't communicate.

1. Try saying, "I heard you had a rough day yesterday. When you want to talk about it, let me know," or "I have some new ideas about the problem you had the other day. Let me know when you have time to hear them."

2. Walk away.

Eventually these children will come to talk about the problem, but on their own timetable, not on yours. Walking away gives them power because you have respected what they say they want. Acknowledging that a problem did occur also lets them know that you are not going to ignore or deny difficulties. Some of these children adopt this style to gain power through withholding. They fear that talking with someone will mean that person will take control of their lives. Helplessness terrifies them. Others use this style because they honestly cannot communicate about feelings—their own or others. Refusing to communicate protects their secret and doesn't reveal their vulnerabilities or lack of skill and ability to communicate. If a child persists in not communicating, seek a third party to help start the conversation.

For the Externalizer

Try these strategies with the child who blames someone else.

1. Let your child know that you know what happened.

2. Listen to the entire description of the experience from your child's perspective without interruption. Then calmly ask, "What was your part?"

3. Label any feelings that are shared with an empathic response, such as, "Looks like you are really struggling."

4. Without passing judgment, point out that there may be long-range consequences to be experienced even if it was the other child's fault.

5. Say, "I may not have the right answer, but I'd be happy to talk about it so you don't find yourself in trouble later."

6. Help your child have a realistic assessment of the situation, not an over-dramatized one. Ask, "What's the worst that could happen?"

7. Be creative and start a dialogue about possible solutions and intervention plans. Try to suggest some that are humorous, fun, or engaging rather than power positions. Support any healthy intervention ideas your child comes up with.

Many of these children avoid exposing themselves and their feelings at all costs. Some are truly lacking in insight. They most sincerely see the onset of all problems as something done to them. This is a risky position to take in life because it eliminates the necessity for dialoguing and problem-solving. Believing that others are always at fault takes away personal responsibility for problem-solving. Many of these are the children who get into serious trouble later in life in relationships and in jobs. They cannot get along with people because they cannot own their own part in creating difficult social situations. It is tempting to insist that these children see their own part in creating the problem and to punish them to teach a lesson. Don't do either because it only deepens the sense of alienation and estrangement that they feel. The key to solving the problem is in building and modeling a positive relationship, establishing trust, and creating opportunities for these children to experience intimacy and the rewards that come with a healthy relationship. Your initial goal must be a simple one—simply build communication, shared feelings, and a plan for solving a problem in a way that doesn't mean being cruel to another person.

There is another type of child who falls into this category. This child blames others—usually the bully, but possibly also the victim—while often failing to recognize that he or she has a choice to follow the lead of the bully or not. The bully's place in the power structure is important to this type of child. By aligning with or acting on behalf of the bully, the child reduces his or her anxiety about being targeted. In doing this, however, he or she sacrifices a sense of personal choice and becomes linked to a poor model—a model who uses put-downs, cruelty, and intimidation to get what he or she wants from others. To promote feelings of safety *and* efficacy with this type of child, help him or her develop the skills to dialogue with others, gain the respect of others, and achieve power through strength of character. For these children, the first step is to build self-awareness. The ultimate goal is one of creating individual solutions separate from those created by the bully. Learning not to follow the crowd, but to think independently, is the behavior to shape. The more you can engage your child in creative problem-solving with you, the better off he or she will be in identifying better choices.

For the Child Beyond Hope

Try these strategies for the child who believes there is nothing anyone can do to help.

1. Listen carefully for the following as your child talks about the bullying situation. Does he or she exhibit any of the following?

   - a very high degree of fear

   - a strong sense of helplessness and hopelessness

   - a sense that no one can possibly help or change the situation sadness

   - a loss of interest in school

   - a sense of no friends

2. If your child is feeling some of the above, be compassionate and communicate that there is hope.

3. Reassure your child that when bullying problems get this out of hand, it takes a team approach to solve them.

4. Let your child know that you are going to work with him or her every step of the way to think through a comprehensive plan.

5. Break the problem down into pieces, and address each separately to make the situation less overwhelming.

Creating such a plan might involve a number of steps that will need to be worked through together and possibly with others. For example, it may involve:

- approaching the right person at the school and asking for help in changing the climate of the school

- finding some friends to feel safe with

- finding a counselor to help with the feelings of sadness

- joining a group to work on social skills

These children are often so defeated and hopeless about the bullying problems that they believe no help is possible. They suffer silently and live each day at school with a great deal of fear. School or the activity in which the bullying occurs is no longer fun or of any interest to them. The social environment has become so miserable that enjoyment is no longer possible.

There is a difference between hopeless children and whiny children. Hopeless children may not even have the energy to convey a long list of complaints. They often have given up all hope that change is possible. Attempting to encourage them to assert themselves or stand up for their rights will be futile because they don't have the energy or self-confidence to muster the effort.

It is critically important that you convey a sense of hope to your child and that you demonstrate interventions on his or her behalf. Until some margin of safety is felt at school, some friends found, and better feelings built, your child will not be capable of learning, much less using the protective and coping skills presented in earlier chapters. Gradually, you and a counselor can introduce these. If the sense of sadness does not begin to change as the environment improves, you may need to consider a stronger course of action. Finding a competent child mental health professional, preferably one familiar with bullying problems, may truly be a favor to this child. This extent of sadness should not be part of childhood, and outside help can often support you as a parent in relieving these feelings for your child. Also consider a change of schools or programs, as discussed earlier; some children have been so severely bullied that the image of being the victim just cannot be changed in their current school environment.

Chapter 15

What if Your Child Is The Bully?
Developing Positive Power

If you recognize that you may be the parent of a bully, congratulations. Most parents refuse to even think about this possibility; they are certain the victim provoked and their child simply retaliated back. In some ways, this is accurate in that slightly more than 50 percent of children who bully were also targeted at some point in time. Most report experiencing this during the middle school years and some retaliate with violence, others with social manipulation, cyberbullying or threats. Power dynamics play a critical role and they constantly shift in middle school and high school as teens jostle for social status. Bullying is one avenue to the top of the hierarchy. Help your child see that he or she can gain power and recognition through acts of kindness and compassion. And start teaching this message early so that your child has a battery of well-honed skills that can be used in the middle and high school years.

Pay attention if you are alerted that your child has bullied as the long term outcome for children who are not redirected is quite dire. Bullies are at high risk for relationship difficulties and felony convictions by young adulthood.

Be especially worried if your child displays any of the traits below:

- Lacks compassion and empathy
- Seems clueless and truly unaware of how his or her behavior might feel to others
- Seems to always place his or her needs above those of others
- Is cruel and seems to feel pleasure when hurting others
- Is determined to win at all costs
- Cannot regulate anger and quickly reacts with physical aggression or very hurtful words

The earlier you recognize these traits and intervene, the better. The early childhood years are when children develop empathy and build friendships. These years are critical for stopping aggressive behavior, the use of unkind words, and the insistence on having one's own way. From the earliest interactions with others, parents must have conversations with their children often about school, activities, and how to treat others. Developing empathy and expressing anger without harming others are primary skills parents must address upon learning that their child has bullied. The earlier risks are recognized and minimized, the more likely a child can learn to replace the satisfaction felt by using power to intimidate and harm with other healthier behaviors.

Having been abused or bullied with no safe haven is a significant red flag. Supporting a child with these risk factors and replacing harmful interactions with empathic protection is essential. Channeling reactive and aggressive tendencies early in development with emotional regulation is critical. If your child displays the risk factors listed above, professional intervention will probably be needed to shape the best course of treatment.

Equally important is recognizing that the social environment of the school is a key factor in shaping children with impulse control difficulties, aggressive tendencies or highly reactive temperament. Using the climate evaluation found in Chapter 5 determine if the school is a helpful or harmful fit for your child's temperament. Is the school one of high competitiveness, are disciplinary techniques that discourage bullying and put-downs lacking, does your child have adults with whom to build trust and respect, are his or her interests represented? Schools are shaped by their size, turn over, inclusivity or exclusivity, hidden cultures that leave little or no room for personal expression, too much or too little structure, and use of cooperative versus competitive learning. Look at the dynamics in the school classroom. Are problem solving techniques employed, is there an equalization of power, do teachers help resolve conflicts or are contexts present that create bullying with minimal responsiveness from the teacher?

There are classroom and school contexts that allow bullying to flourish.

What can the family do?

1. Listen to your child and ask yourself if you model problem-solving in your own life.

2. Teach your child about mutuality and the give and take of friendships.

3. Work together on apologies, owning up to mistreatment of others, and the consequences of winning at all costs.

4. Help your child to identify anger and frustration. Provide words and acceptable actions to express these emotions.

5. Point out and discuss how aggression is displayed in the media.

6. Use stories from the news, websites, books, or even fables to discuss ways to problem solve.

7. Read to younger children; there are many good children's books that address bullying on the market today. Refer to the Resources List.

8. Channel the child's desire for power into healthy ways to be powerful, such as positive leadership, building on interests and strengths, community service, and upstander behaviors.

9. Change schools if there is a problematic fit between your child's temperament and the social environment of the school or classroom.

A child who relishes power, lacks empathy and/or has anger control issues will not learn management, self-regulation or develop healthy friendships in a school environment that is a mismatch for his or her basic high risk temperament.

Some children who bully have natural leadership skills but do not have the self-control or any models for directing these skills in a positive direction. If this describes your child, point out the status and power enjoyed by upstanders. Some therapists, as well as some schools, offer groups in social skills that model positive activism, how to stand up for others, and become involved in addressing social injustices.

Chapter 16

Shaping a Bystander into an Upstander

Bystanders are the children who know about the bullying. They either watch it firsthand or hear about it through others. A large percentage of children (85%) are bystanders. They are not targets. They are not bullies. Later in life they often report feeling guilty for not doing anything to help the victim or for joining in when they knew it was wrong. Over the years, researchers (Rivers, 2012) have confirmed that these children are emotionally impacted with guilt, anxiety and fear. Why, you may wonder, do children just watch helplessly as another child is tormented? The reasons vary for different temperaments.

Some children gain social status themselves by participating. These children are often referred to as lieutenants or confederates, and encourage or prod the bully on, laughing or cheering, or just being an audience. Bullies like an audience as it confirms the power that accompanies the gratification from putting down another.

Friends may entice your child into bullying others. It takes courage to stand up for another child when there is social pressure to join in. You can explore with your child how much he or she can risk in order to help. Even small actions can make a big difference. Some children cannot take a stand alone. It feels too frightening and threatening, but they may be able to join in if another child goes first and sets the trend.

Other children avoid any action because they are terrified that the bully may turn on them and they do not want to direct any attention to themselves. Finally, there are the children who hide or isolate to protect themselves. Sadly, in the long run, bullying takes a toll on all children who witnesses hurtful behavior but do nothing to assert their power in a positive and caring way to stop it.

Empowering your child to become an upstander, which means taking some sort of action, benefits everyone. Indeed, shaping a bystander into an upstander is the backbone of promoting positive school climate. More than half of the time, bullying stops within ten seconds if a bystander does something (Craig & Pepler, 1997). Yet only one in five children spontaneously intervenes (Rigby, 2007). Interestingly, elementary aged students are more likely to do something than high school aged students, yet both age groups report that they know they should do something. What, then, can a parent do to encourage a child to shift from being a bystander to an upstander?

- Explain the serious difference between tattling and telling. When someone is being hurt, it is not tattling to help keep another person safe.

- Acknowledge that confronting the bully is scary but telling an identified trusted adult is typically not too emotionally frightening for most children.

- Some schools and communities have hot lines where a student can call in a concern anonymously. Find out what is available in your community.

- Suggest that the child can offer an escape for the targeted person, or support him or her afterwards by saying, "I saw what happened and it was not fair," or "We do not talk to people that way at our school." Be a friend/upstander.

- Practice strategies to use for different situations. Role play often benefits children more than discussion alone.

- Talk to your child about engaging others to join in upstanding behavior. It is much easier to confront bullying behavior when the climate of the school is set by a majority of students joining together to set a tone of safety for all.

- Model how to use respectful language and do not, yourself, insult someone by stereotyping people based on race, mental capacity, sexual orientation, physical characteristics, religion, or ethnicity.

- Observe your child carefully to see if he or she is numb to violence or hurtful behavior inflicted on others or incapable of empathy. Discuss real life examples and explore what feelings were evoked. If you do not detect some capacity to identify with the victim(s), your child may need professional help as this is a serious predictor of later relationship difficulties.

Skills for Life

Most children are bystanders. These children know what is happening, who is being bullied and, later in life, often report feeling guilty for not doing anything to help or for joining in when they knew it was wrong.

Friends may entice your child into bullying others. It takes courage to stand up for another child when there is social pressure to join in. You can explore with your child how much he or she can risk in order to help. Some children cannot take a stand alone. It feels too frightening, but joining with a group that takes a stand is less threatening. Many schools, today, are working toward the creation of a caring community, which is a group of students and adults who are committed to creating a caring, respectful, and inclusive learning environment that is physically, emotionally, intellectual and socially safe for all students. These schools honor children who move from being bystanders to upstanders.

Even if your child's school does not have such a program, there are a number of ways to help. Some carry more risk than others. Look over the table, Levels of Risk, on page 120 and consider what fits your child's style and the situations he or she may observe. Not every idea is for every child. Remember, however, that doing something is better than doing nothing. Sometimes only one child has the courage to do what is fair, and then, surprisingly, others join in. These strategies or ideas carry different levels of risk. Some are safe and comfortable for most children, whereas others require extraordinary courage and leadership skill. Do not push your child into a position or risk he or she is not ready to take. Find the right one. Courage and character strength build slowly over time and across many situations.

Five different strategies are identified. Each has a level of risk that ranges from low to high. Most children are capable of low risk. Many children just don't think of or consider these ideas. Share them with your child and practice how to use them in real-life situations. Help your child create a plan that works well for him or her.

Levels of Risk

Strategies of Intervention	Low ⟵		High ⟶
Not Joining In	Walk away.	Stay but do not participate.	Declare your nonparticipation.
Getting Adult Help	Get help anonymously.	Identify who the helpful adults are and get one of them.	Announce loudly your intention to get adult help; then do it.
Mobilizing Peer Group	Identify a peer leader and offer to join in standing up to the bully.	Identify others who are capable of mobilizing peers in defense of the target and recruit them to the cause.	Be a leader in recruiting others to join in standing up to the bully.
Taking an Individual Stand	Go over to the target and lead him or her away from the situation.	Say, "Leave him/her alone."	Say, "We don't treat people like that at our school."
Befriending the Target	Privately empathize with the target by saying, "That was unfair or cruel."	Go over and stand with the target or invite him or her to join you in doing something else.	Stand with the target and publicly announce the "unfair" behavior of the bully.

Closing

This book has introduced an array of simple tools and resources to help you better understand your child's temperament, vulnerabilities, and school climate. It has also provided guidance in developing effective strategies for addressing bullying when it occurs. The authors recognize that bully-proofing your child can be a challenging task, but with some patience, focus, and the right tools, you and others in your community will be able to create an environment in which all children feel safe and can thrive. Partner with school personnel who share your belief in a positive school environment.

"Safety and security don't just happen, they are the result of collective consensus and public investment. We owe our children, the most vulnerable citizens in our society, a life free of violence and fear."

– Nelson Mandela

Websites

http://cyberbullying.us The Cyberbullying Research Center's website is regularly updated with information, tools, and research on online harassment.

http://www.stopbullying.gov This is a government website with information from the Department of Education and the Department of Health and Human Services on preventing bullying. This site has information, definitions, prevention ideas as well as intervention strategies. There is a special section devoted to children with disabilities and special needs.

http://www.commonsensemedia.org This site explores technology and media literacy, highlighting opportunities and pitfalls. Lessons, as applicable to home as to school, are available from kindergarten through high school.

http://www.partnershipuniversity.org Click on "Getting Serious: A Best Practice Approach to Bullying Prevention." This is a 10-12 hour self-directed course that provides an overview of bullying concepts, deepens understanding about school climate and educates about specific topics related to bullying such as religion, sexual orientation, gender expression, and cyberbullying. There is also a much shorter online guide specifically for parents.

http://www.pacer.org/bullying Pacer is an organization for parents of children with disabilities. Their National Bullying Prevention Center provides digital resources for parents, schools, teens and youth.

Books for Adults

Bullied: What Every Parent, Teacher, and Kid Needs to Know About Ending the Cycle of Fear by Carrie Goldman

Bullying in North American Schools by Dorothy Espelage and Susan Swearer

Bullying In Schools and What to Do About It by Ken Rigby

Bullying in Sports: A Guide to Identifying the Injuries We Don't See by Randy Nathan

Bullying: A Handbook for Educators and Parents by Ian Rivers, Neil Duncan and Valerie Besag

Bullying Prevention: What Parents Need to Know by Wendy Craig, Debra Pepler and Joanne Cummings

Bully-Proofing Your School by Carla Garrity, William Porter, Nancy Sager, Kathryn Jens and Cam Short-Camilli

How Children Succeed by Paul Tough.

Little Girls Can Be Mean by Michelle Anthony and Reyna Lindert

lol...OMG!: What Every Student Needs to Know About Online Reputation Management, Digital Citizenship and Cyberbullying by Matt Ivester

Odd Girl Out: The Hidden Culture of Aggression in Girls by Rachel Simmons

Queen Bees and Wannabees: Helping Your Daughter Survive Cliques, Gossip, Boyfriends, and the New Realities of Girl World by Rosalind Wiseman

Sticks and Stones: Defeating the Culture of Bullying and Rediscovering the Power of Character and Empathy by Emily Bazelon

Talking Back to Facebook: The Common Sense Guide to Raising Kids in the Digital Age by James Steyer

The Bully, the Bullied, and the Bystanders by Barbara Colorosa

The New Bully Free Classroom; Proven Prevention and Intervention Strategies for Teachers K-8 by Allan Beane

Books for Younger Children

Bailey and the Big Bully by Liz Boyd

Chrysanthemum by Kevin Henkes

Don't Squeal Unless It Is a Big Deal: A Tale of Tattletales by Jeannie Franz Ransom

How to Lose All Your Friends by Nancy Carlson

King of the Playground by Phyllis Reynolds Naylor

Oliver Button is a Sissy by Tomie dePaola

One by Kathryn Otoshi

Simon's Hook: A Story About Teases and Put-downs by Karen Gedig Burnett

Stop Picking on Me by Pat Thomas

Tattlin Madeline by Carol Cummings

The Juice Box Bully: Empowering Kids to Stand Up for Others by Bob Sornson and Maria Dismondy

The Recess Queen by Alexis O'Neill

Books for Older Children

Bullies Are a Pain in the Brain by Trevor Romain

Bully by Patricia Polacco

Cliques, Phoneys and Other Baloney by Trevor Romain

Confessions of a Former Bully by Trudy Ludwig

Hundred Dresses by Eleanor Estes

Please Stop Laughing at Me by Jodee Blanco

Stand Up For Yourself and Your Friends: Dealing with Bullies and Bossiness and Finding a Better Way by Patti Criswell and Angela Martini

Wonder by R J Palacio

References

Center for Social and Emotional Education (2010, January). *School climate research summary:* (Issue Brief **Vol. 1, No. 1**) New York, NY: Cohen, J. & Geier, V. K.

Craig, W., & Pepler, D. (1997). Observations of bullying and victimization in the schoolyard. *Canadian Journal of School Psychology. 2,* 41–60.

Crick, N.R., & Grotpeter, J.K. (1995). Relational aggression, gender, and social-psychological adjustment. *Child Development, 66*(3), 710–722.

Garrity, C., Jens, K., Porter, W., Sager, N., & Short-Camilli, C. (1994.) *Bully Proofing Your School: A Comprehensive Approach for Elementary Schools.* Longmont, CO: Sopris West Educational Services.

Heck, N. C., Flentje, A., & Cochran, B. N. (2011). Offsetting risks: high school gay-straight alliances and lesbian, gay, bisexual, and transgender (LGBT) youth." *School Psychology Quarterly.* Advance online publication. doi: 10.1037/a0023226

Rigby, K. (2007). *Bullying in schools and what to do about it* (Updated, revised), Melbourne, Australian: Council for Education Research.

Rivers, I. (2012). Morbidity among bystanders of bullying behavior at school: concepts, concerns, and clinical/research issues. *International Journal of Adolescent Medicine and Health.* doi:10.1515/ijamh.2012.003

Wilson, D. (2004). The interface of school climate and school connectedness and relationships with aggression and victimization. *Journal of School Health, 74*(7), 293-299.

Index

CPSIA information can be obtained
at www.ICGtesting.com
Printed in the USA
FSOW03n2109041115
13003FS